CORELLI

His Life, His Work

Da Capo Press Music Reprint Series

MUSIC EDITOR
BEA FRIEDLAND
Ph.D., City University of New York

MARC PINCHERLE

CORELLI
His Life, His Work

Translated from the French
by Hubert E. M. Russell

DA CAPO PRESS • NEW YORK • 1979

Library of Congress Cataloging in Publication Data

Pincherle, Marc, 1888-1974.
  Corelli: his life, his work.

  (Da Capo Press music reprint series)
  Reprint of the 1956 ed. published by W. W. Norton,
New York.
  Includes bibliographies and index.
  1. Corelli, Arcangelo, 1653-1713. 2. Composers—
Italy—Biography.
[ML410.C78P52 1979] 787'.1'0924 [B]   79-9155
ISBN 0-306-79576-0

Published by Da Capo Press, Inc.
A Subsidiary of Plenum Publishing Corporation
227 West 17th Street, New York, N.Y. 10011

CORELLI

His Life, His Work

MARC PINCHERLE

CORELLI
His Life, His Work

Translated from the French
by Hubert E. M. Russell

W · W · NORTON & COMPANY · INC · *New York*

Contents

Illustrations

Preface

THE PRESENT work is the free reshaping of a *Corelli* which I published a little more than twenty years ago. In the meantime, the biographical data have not been modified to any considerable degree, except with reference to the legend of the journey to Paris, and I hope to establish the inanity of this. On the other hand, the work has benefited by new elucidations: there is a better discernment of Corelli's decisive influence in the elaboration of preclassical instrumental art and, consequently, of all modern instrumental music.

For some time now historians devoted to the study of the period with which we are concerned (*ca.* 1675–*ca.* 1715) have ceased to be hypnotised by the single figure of J. S. Bach who until recently was considered as embodying all previous evolution and bearing all futurity within himself. A start has been made to render justice to some precursors, among whom the Italians were of prime importance in respect to all that was germane to forms originally inspired by the bowed instruments: sonata, symphony, and concerto.

Thus one comes to study these Italians with enhanced interest. And not merely through the printed page. In 1933 I wrote: "The name of Corelli has retained an impressive fame

across the centuries; the cult devoted to him from the day
of his death remains intact. Now his work, though easy to
appreciate and most grateful to perform, is practically neglected; in contemporary musical life there is heard but now
and then one concerto from the twelve (invariably the same
one, the eighth) and a few violin solos, generally transcribed
and almost as often misrepresented." Today these lines would
be a flagrant injustice. Although the programs of too many
virtuosi persist in embracing calamitous disarrangements of
the *follia*, still, authentic Corellian sonatas are being played,
and with increasing frequency.

But the happiest turn of fortune lies in the restoration to
the repertoire of the concerti grossi, Opus VI. The growing
fashion of chamber orchestras, many of which, particularly
in Italy, specialize in music of the eighteenth century, helps
the movement, which is reinforced by the record industry.
A complete recording of Opus VI has just been issued, and
from all appearances this will be followed by others.

On the tercentenary of Corelli's birth we no longer merely
admire a conventional portrait of him taken on trust. His
work regains its living colors. The case can be judged from
his compositions: the panegyric is less necessary than ever
before. I have endeavored in my writing not to lose sight of
this fact.

To conclude, may I reiterate the expression of gratitude
which I paid in 1933 to musicians and musicologists by whom
I was favored with invaluable aid: Charles Van den Borren,
Alfred Cortot, Guido M. Gatti, Dr. Robert Haas, Dr. Carlo
Piancastelli, the staffs of the Music Section of the British
Museum, of the libraries of the Universities of Turin and Up-

sala, and of the *Gesellschaft der Musikfreunde*, Vienna; and to those, now, to my regret, deceased—F. T. Arnold, Alberto Cametti, Alfred Einstein, Francesco Vatielli, and Miss Marion Scott.

This redrafting has benefited from the light shed on pre-classical instrumental music, in the interim, by Suzanne Clercx, Manfred Bukofzer, Hans Engel, Paul Henry Lang, Bernhard Paumgartner, and William C. Smith. And I have received directly from Mme. Elisabeth Lebeau and my con-frères, Andrea Della Corte, François Lesure, and Claudio Sartori, interesting particulars for which I would ask them to be so gracious as to herein find my sincere thanks.

There was little to be culled from the voluminous *Corelli* by Mario Rinaldi; I have accounted for my position in various reviews of this work.

M. P.

CORELLI

His Life, His Work

I

The Life of Corelli

P RIOR TO 1600 instrumental music had some inclinations to lead an existence independent of vocal polyphony; but its real taking wing dates from the opening of the seventeenth century, and its point of departure was Italy.

Just when a new spirit was substituting accompanied monody for the counterpoint of the renaissance, when opera was being born, when the major-minor tonality was asserting the hegemony which was to reign uncontested throughout the classical and romantic eras, the art of stringed instrument construction achieved a decisive advance, virtually in one bound carrying to their point of perfection the violin and its acolytes, the viola, violoncello, and double bass. Specifically instrumental forms were roughed out whose progress was to be extraordinarily rapid. After the first stutterings of the sonata as far back as 1620, important composers—Biagio Marini, Massimiliano Neri, Tarquinio Merula—established its structure, at the same time elaborating the techniques of appropriate performance.

With certain of them, technical invention took precedence over purely musical preoccupations. They became inebriated with their discoveries. There were to be seen taking shape in the work of Carlo Farini and later in the work of Marco Uccellini premonitory signs of acrobatic virtuosity, which so easily encroaches when left with a free field. So that about 1675 the need made itself felt in all spheres—form, texture, technique—of a factor of unification, and, at least provisionally, of stabilization (the time to get organized on solid foundations), and of a model who would compel recognition on the part of all these scattered pioneers—a *chef d'école*. At that opportune moment entered the musician competent above all others to assume this role: Arcangelo Corelli.

He was born on the 17th of February, 1653, at Fusignano, an ancient city of the lower Romagna, in the diocese of Faenza, midway between Bologna and Ravenna.[1]

His family were numbered among the oldest and wealthiest of the town. A long time before the birth of Arcangelo certain genealogists of the Corelli had averred that they came from Rome in 1405 and were descendants of Coriolanus—a daring assertion, the temerity of which has, however, been surpassed: Zabarella, the author of a *Corelio* published at Padua in 1664, having to trace back the origins of the powerful house of Correr of Venice, affiliated it to the Corelli of Rome, for whom he contrived descent in direct line through the kings of Paphlagonia from Japhet, son of Noah!

Local traditions relating to the acts and sayings of the Corelli during the Middle Ages and the beginning of the Renaissance present them to us as athirst for domination, turbulent, swift to revolt. No doubt it is necessary to discriminate in all that has been laid to their charge. For example, in the middle of the 15th century the mother of one Bertuzzo Corelli was said to have obtained by intrigue from the Count of Cunio, her seigneur, a vast territory in the Nagajone valley between Fusi-gnano and Ravenna. Now, the authentic title deed has been found in which is recounted the transfer of the aforesaid valley, it having been sold the 30th of September, 1444, in a very proper transaction to Bertuzzo di Tura (Bonaventura) Corelli by Andrea Salutano for the sum of one hundred livres. By this act Bertuzzo became one of the large landed proprietors of the region.

But it is true that much later on, in 1632, scarcely twenty years before the advent of Arcangelo to this world, a Rudolfo Corelli was decapitated and mutilated and the *disjecta membra* strewn before his dwelling for having attempted, at the head of a band of rioters, to kill his overlord Mario Calcagnini. The house was utterly destroyed: the ground whereon it stood was ploughed and sprinkled with salt. Under the sinister name of *Guasto dei Corelli* (The Devastation of the Corellis) the site was to remain deserted until 1753, the year when the abbé Marquise Giulio Corelli gifted it so that the Church *del Pio Suffragio* (Of the Devout Supplication) might be built there. Attention is drawn to these sanguinary events for the singular contrast they offer to what we know of the character of our hero.

The greatest piety, let us add, coexisted with this extreme violence in the family. Of fourteen churches in the territory of Fusignano, half were erected at the expense of the Corelli, except one for which they nevertheless gave the site. Several members of the family entered religious orders. Others made their mark as jurists, mathematicians, and doctors; four Corelli, from the 16th to the 19th century, were no mean poets. Yet there was no musician of stature among them; nothing which explains or gives reason to anticipate a vocation of a virtuoso-composer.

Corelli's youth has prodigiously excited the imagination of his biographers, and a very odd picture may be obtained by aligning the legend with the few historical facts which are known for certain. Without reprinting all the inventions of intrepid improvisers, among whom, however, were some within reach of good sources of information, we will grant a mention, at least, to those of their findings which have retained authority for the longest time.

Here, to start with, is the testimony of the Abbé C. F. Laurenti in his *Storia di Fusignano*, dated 1799–1813, the manuscript of which is kept by the municipality of Fusignano. According to him, the vocation of the infant Corelli was aroused on hearing the priest of his native town play. Another priest, the incumbent of Saint-Savino, is said to have imparted to him the first elements of his art. In order to get lessons Arcangelo is supposed to have gone, in defiance of the inclemencies of the weather, two miles from the paternal roof every day. Now and then in summer, so Laurenti romances, Corelli would perchance rest under a tree. Suddenly inspired he would take up his violin and from it draw forth melodies so beautiful that the folks of the neighborhood would gather in a group around him. Very soon the pupil outstripped his master. The family wishing to persuade him to give up music, a third priest, Corelli's uncle, then intervened and brought it about that, despite the father's wish, the child should be sent to Faenza to study. The result exceeded every expectation: at a concert given on the occasion of a visit of Cardinal Ottoboni, Arcangelo evinced such extraordinary talent that the Cardinal "stood astounded at it." On his return to Rome the Cardinal imbued the Pope with a desire to hear in turn a virtuoso precocious to this degree. The bishop of Faenza was written, at whose instigation the young violinist, overcoming his timidity, made for the pontifical town.

Dr. Carlo Piancastelli has authoritatively disproved this laborious fabrication of impostures. Two manifest falsehoods: no uncle figures as a priest in the family records of the Corelli, and the paternal opposition is hard to reconcile with the patent fact that the young Arcangelo could never have known his father, who died on January 13, 1653, a month before Corelli's birth. It has been established that the widow—née Santa Raffini [2]—brought up to the best of her ability the infant and her four elder children, Ippolito, Domenico, Giovanna, and Giacinto.

It is also known on good authority that at this period the family lived in very easy circumstances, possessing a landed estate which was to remain intact until about the close of the 18th century. As for the house where Corelli was born, it is believed that it was situated in the southern quarter of Fusignano on the present site of the Villa Severoli.

In respect to Corelli's youthful years, we do have evidence worthy of credence: that of Crescimbeni, who had seen and known Corelli, his colleague at the *Accademia dei Arcadi*. He tells us that Arcangelo, when quite young, had been sent to Faenza "where he received from a priest the first rudiments of music (*del suono*). He continued to study it at Lugo, then at Bologna, though it was not intended that he should make it his profession. But the violin moved Corelli with passion, so much so that he decided to devote himself to it entirely, and he remained four years at Bologna."

Working with the testimonies of Crescimbeni and Padre Martini, Francesco Vatielli has managed to define with precision the Bolognese influences [3] on Corelli. Perhaps it is unwarranted to deduce from the passage quoted from Crescimbeni, especially from his words *"del suono,"* that the composer received only a theoretical initiation at Faenza, and that he only began the study of the violin at Bologna in 1666, being then thirteen years old. But it is conjecturable that there alone did he apply himself to it in a methodical way; anyhow his progress was so rapid that the *Accademia Filarmonica*, which was already celebrated, accepted him in 1670, when he was barely seventeen.

The School of Bologna was then in its heyday: we shall return later to its particular merits and to that which it could contribute to the formation of a young talent. May we just refer to the masters to whom Corelli turned, and whose names are revealed by a manuscript note of Padre Martini. The first chronologically is Giovanni Benvenuti of Bologna, a member of the *Accademia Filarmonica*. With this follower of Ercole Gaïbara, the true founder of the first Bolognese School of the violin, Corelli acquired in particular, so far as we can tell, the elements of his technique. He then perfected himself musically with another pupil of the same Gaïbara, the Venetian Leonardo Brugnoli, an accomplished and inspired violinist especially famous for his gifts as an improviser, according to Padre Martini. Conscious of what he owed to them, Corelli deemed it a point of honor, once he was in Rome, to assert his artistic affiliation:

on the title page of his first three works he is *"Arcangelo Corelli da Fusignano, detto il Bolognese."*

The English historian Dr. Burney also mentions (III, 548) a Roman tradition according to which Corelli is supposed to have been the pupil of Bartolomeo Girolamo Laurenti at Bologna. Rinaldi disputes this; but comparisons which Francesco Vatielli [4] has made between passages from the sonatas for solo violin and bass of Laurenti published at Bologna in 1691, and others selected from Opus V of Corelli published in 1700, lend considerable plausibility to Burney's claim.

It is seen that there has not been any question at all about Bassani, whom the historians had designated until these last few years as being the teacher of Corelli. It is Bassani whom Ernst Ortlepp presents to us, under the name of Bassini, in a really extravagant account the purpose of which it is difficult to grasp.[5] The aforesaid "old violinist Giambattista Bassini" takes the young Corelli as a pupil toward the end of 1670. Bassini has a daughter with whom the adolescent falls desperately in love: to induce him to propose she coquettes with another fellow pupil, the Marquis of Monteserrato, who is nettled into response, becomes enamored, and succeeds in winning her hand. Corelli flees in despair: but later he rejoins the cruel one, subdues her, and receives from her illicit favors. Separation. Thirty-five years later he finds himself one fine day in the presence of the princess Casarini in whom he recognizes his own daughter, born of his amours with the marchioness. Unbending in her pride, she gives him a frigid reception, feigns ignorance of the bond between them—and the poor father dies of chagrin.

The "old Bassini," or rather Bassani, would have been thirteen years old when Corelli entered on his eighteenth year: the most audacious authors of novelized lives would recoil from such a coup de grâce to chronology.

Before the real masters of Corelli had been identified, Antoine Vidal had observed very judiciously the improbability of the tradition which, without going to the fictional excess of Ortlepp, established the relation of master and pupil between the two violinists. "Bassani, born about 1657, was then younger than Corelli," wrote Vidal, "and we find it hard to conceive that he could have been sufficiently precocious in his talent to give lessons to a pupil like himself." [6] Arnold Schering touches on an explanation which ought at least to be advanced with reservations. He mentions certain stylistic features which attest the influence that the Venetian opera of Cavalli, Cesti, and Legrenzi may have exercised over Corelli. From these he deduces that the young master "himself has probably studied at Venice in company with Bassani." But nothing positive has ever revealed Corelli's presence at any time whatsoever in the city of the Doges; nor, moreover, was Bassani ever to be encountered there, except for the period of his earliest youth when he studied with the priest Castrovillari.

If permissible doubt remains on this score, there is no longer any in respect to another journey opportunely invented to close a gap in the life story of Corelli. It is known that the stay of Corelli at Bologna lasted four years, from 1666 to 1670, after which his trace is lost for a time. Some historians brought him to Rome as early as 1671. Still, there is no certitude until the beginning of 1675.[7] For the interim we have indeed a sojourn in Paris imagined, not by Hawkins, but by Jean-Jacques

Rousseau in his *Lettre sur la Musique françoise* of 1753, where it was stated: "Lully himself, alarmed by the arrival of Correlli in France, hastened to have him expelled from France: which was all the more easy for him in so far as Correlli was the greater man, and in consequence less of a sycophant than he." [8] Mainwaring, the historian of Handel, took up this tattle and amplified it: "The advantages which he drew from his acquaintance with Corelli will not be forgot any more than the return which he made by raising a faction against him and driving him from Paris." [9] Hawkins merely followed up, adding the gratuitous details: "His curiosity led him to visit Paris, probably with a view to attend the improvements which they were making in music under the influence of Cardinal Mazarin" (*General History of Music*, 1776, III, 309). Yet this cardinal had already been dead eleven years by 1672! Let us pass over Arteaga, Perotti, and others, to smile at the excessive zeal of Piero Maroncelli when he declares Lully was beholden to Corelli in the matter of musical construction: "If it is then objected that Lully preceded Corelli, remember that Lully and his orchestra, celebrated throughout all Europe, were incapable of performing the sonatas of Corelli in less time than three years study, and then in a mediocre way: that it was only when forty years of age, in 1672, that Lully wrote his first opera in Paris, whither Corelli had just arrived, and had perchance imbued him with the idea of the French overture!"

I am ignoring the embroideries added by Morini, Laurenti, and Fignanani about the triumphant journeys across France, and about the rich marriage proposed to Arcangelo in Paris which he tactfully declined, either from modesty or in order to consecrate himself entirely to his art.

The Gallophobia of Rousseau when music is involved is probably responsible for much ado about nothing: although the so-called Corelli-Lully conflict took place in an age when, according to him, French and Italian music were not very differentiated as yet, there could be noted already among French composers, as Rousseau pontificates—"the germ of that jealousy which is inseparable from inferiority." It is not the Florentine composer he takes to task in Lully, but the creator and champion of French opera, whom he is careful to present in the same *Lettre sur la Musique françoise* as a very humble forerunner: "From the time of Orlande and Goudimel harmony and sounds were made, and to such Lully has added a little cadency; Corelli, Buononcini, Vinci, and Pergolesi are the first to have made music."

The futility of trying to prove that Corelli did journey to Paris is obvious from the facts: no search of the archives has ever revealed anything; contemporary newssheets are silent on the subject, although they were never niggardly with details of the arrival of a foreign musician, such as Westhoff, at Paris; and two musicians—François Couperin and Georg Muffat—who wrote much on their art and who professed the liveliest admiration for Lully and for Corelli, never made the least reference to an encounter between them. And how is it to be explained that a *mélomane* as informed as Titon du Tillet does not allude to it when he comes to speak of the artistic affinities of the two masters: "I have heard it said to a gentleman in waiting of the late Cardinal d'Estrées and to Baptiste (Anet), one of our greatest violinists, that this cardinal, when in Rome, praised Corelli for the beautiful composition of his Sonatas; the latter said to him: Monseigneur, this is because I have studied Lully." [10] In support of this can be adduced the reply that Pierre de Morand made to J. J. Rousseau in the year following the publication of the *Lettre sur la Musique françoise:* "The famous Correlly whose judgment is worth more than that of Monsieur Rousseau was imbued with so much admiration for Lully that he had several works of this great man put into gold frames, and he kept them in his Study like a precious treasure that they might serve him as models. They passed on his death to the house of Ottoboni." [11]

I have felt obliged to dwell on this episode, which so manifestly has been invented, because the most recent biographer of Corelli, Mario Rinaldi, asserts its actuality,[12] and, without advancing the least proof, harps on it inordinately.

As a matter of fact, all this farrago becomes clear if one concedes a reading error on the part of Rousseau, or his copyist or printer, something highly possible eighty-one years after the event in question: *Corelli* being misread for *Cavalli.*

In 1660 Cavalli had certainly arrived in Paris, having been summoned by Mazarin; his presence was enough to disquiet Lully, who was anxious to consolidate his annexation of French opera. Till then Lully had only written ballets: whereas Cavalli had some thirty operas to his credit and was esteemed the first operatic composer of the peninsula, if not of all Christendom. Furthermore, Lully intrigued against Cavalli to the extent of making him return to Venice after two years. Granting that Lully was capable of taking offence at a rival of this caliber, yet how could the young Corelli, in 1672, have provoked his thunderbolts—a violinist of nineteen years, quite unknown in France, who had published nothing and had no aspiration towards opera?

It seems sure then that Rousseau must be indicted for a slip
of the pen, or for some malevolent intention which the context
of the *Lettre sur la Musique françoise* entitles us to ascribe to
him.

It may be that we must needs renounce our desire to know
exactly where the few years were spent following the departure from Bologna. Padre Martini tell us that the young virtuoso stayed for a short time at Fusignano, "but resolved, in order
to assuage the ardent desire he had to go thither and to yield
to the pressing solicitations of numerous and dear friends. . . .
to repair to Rome, where he put himself under the direction
of the famous Pietro Simonelli, from whom he learned with
great facility the fundamentals of counterpoint, thanks to
which he became an excellent and accomplished composer." [13]
It is stated that about this time (1671) he was a violinist at the
theatre of Tor di Nona which had reopened after having been
refurbished through the good offices of Comte d'Alibert,
factotum of Christina of Sweden. But it is only in 1675 that
his presence in Rome is confirmed for us by irrefutable documents.

Alberto Cametti has had the good fortune to unearth the
list of musicians who by their talent gave distinction to the
offices celebrated at the festival of Saint Louis in the church
of Saint-Louis-des-Français at Rome. These ceremonies, of a
most solemn nature, "comprised High Mass and Vespers, the
25th of August, with singing of the first Vespers the eve before, at which foreign ministers, ambassadors, nobility, national clergy, and numerous cardinals were present." [14]

At the beginning of 1675 we find the name of Arcangelo
Corelli appearing as the third of four violinists, with emolu-

ments of one and a half écus, or about eight gold francs, for the three services. The following year he moved up one place. The accounts for August, 1677, do not mention him. He is found again in 1678 as second violin. Second disappearance from 1679 to 1681. Nevertheless, on the 6th of January, 1679, he conducted the orchestra of the Teatro Capranica for the première of a work by his friend Bernardo Pasquini, *Dove è amore è pietà*, the composer being at the harpsichord. Doubtless the Abbé Raguenet recollected this when he wrote: "I have seen at Rome, playing in the same opera, Corelli, Pasquini, and Gaëtani, who are assuredly the world's foremost performers on the violin, the harpsichord, and the theorbo or archlute: moreover these are persons to each of whom is given three or four hundred pistoles a month or six weeks at the most." [15]

A letter addressed by Corelli from Rome on the 3rd of June of the same year to Count Fabrizio Laderchi, offering an unpublished sonata especially composed for him, proves that his stay there was prolonged. His disappearance from the lists of Saint-Louis-des-Français at the beginning of August may possibly mean that one of his journeys to Germany took place during this same summer.

The composer Kaspar Printz claimed to have made Corelli's acquaintance at Munich in 1680.[16] This sketchy evidence—embellished with an inaccuracy, since Printz also affirmed that the young Italian master had already published "some attractive pieces"—constitutes, along with a misconstruction in the biography of Pisendel by Johann Adam Hiller, the sole known source of the more circumstantial accounts according to which Corelli "was appreciated by virtue of his merits by numerous princely courts, and especially at that of the Prince Elector of

Bavaria, who had him in his service for some time." [17] It is not impossible that Corelli likewise stayed at Heidelburg and at Ansbach, where the Elector Palatine maintained an orchestra; and that, as Chrysander claims,[18] he lingered at Hanover in the company of his friend Farinelli, a violinist of repute, from whom he perhaps borrowed the idea of variations on the famous theme of *Folies d'Espagne*, published in 1684 by Playford under the title of "Faronnell's Ground."

But nothing of this is proved. Historian and musicians have frequently gone through the archives at these alleged German residences of Corelli without finding in them the least trace of his peregrination. Better still, the late Dr. Alfred Einstein published the accounts and letters pertaining to art, completely covering this period, of the princes of the Rhine Palatinate. The engagements of virtuosi appear in these papers with all details regarding preliminary negotiations, their emoluments, obligations, and prerogatives.[19] The name of Corelli figures in these archives in 1708—in what context will be seen later— but no allusion to an old friendship nor to any sojourn of the virtuoso at the court of Düsseldorf is to be found.

Therefore, Dr. Einstein was constrained to see pure fictions in these accounts of travels in Germany, fictions for which Printz may have been involuntarily responsible by having erroneously printed the surname Corelli as a substitute for that of Torelli.[20] (It will be seen later that the biographers of Pisendel have confounded the two masters in a like manner.) This flimsy evidence, and perhaps the fact that Opera V and VI are dedicated to German princes, may have touched off the imagination of Arthur Pougin and his associates.

From indubitable evidence we again find Corelli at Rome in

1681: he published there in 1681 his first work of trios, which he dedicated to Christina of Sweden.

The Eternal City was then in a turmoil of social events. Noble houses were rivals in magnificence when it came to putting on comedies or operas, or in producing virtuosi.

Amidst patrons like Prince Ruspoli, the Constable Colonna, the Rospigliosi, Cardinal Savelli, and the Duchess of Bracciano, Christina of Sweden had, despite her abdication, retained a sovereign influence. Her originality, independence of character, and brisk intelligence—she had earlier been dubbed the Pallas Nordica—counted for much in this respect; so did her extraordinary aptitude for disbursing the revenue of provinces the management of which she had retained for herself upon ceding power, which in good years brought her in the equivalent of a million gold francs. A coterie of savants, men of letters, and musicians collected round her at the Palazzo Riario (at that time the seat of the *Accademia dei Lincei*), where she had set up in residence in July, 1659. She installed her magnificent collections there which she had brought away from Stockholm after her abdication, taking them out of their storage at Antwerp. She held musical festivities, and to be admitted to these was deemed a mark of honor. It was probably at such an affair that Moffat, in 1682, heard the concertos of Corelli which impressed him so strongly, and was able to judge the effect of those which he himself had tried to write under the influence of the young master, and in his style.

In August, 1682, Corelli was again to be found at the church of Saint-Louis-des-Français, this time at the head of ten violinists—the orchestra was expanding little by little and a few years later comprised fourteen players—with half an écu increase in pay. By his side, as second violin, was his pupil and friend Matteo Fornari who henceforth was virtually never to leave Corelli. Let us observe in passing that from 1682 to 1708 Corelli was to participate each year as leader of the small orchestra at these festivals of Saint Louis. His earnings were to increase gradually, reaching six écus in 1694. The list for 1709 is lost, and his name was no longer on that of 1710, when he was superseded as first violin by Matteo Fornari.

In January, 1687, James II of England sent the Earl of Castelmain to Rome to negotiate with Pope Innocent XI the return of the three kingdoms to the Catholic faith. Christina of Sweden organized magnificent celebrations in honor of the new ambassador.[21] She offered her guests the première of a cantata by the poet Alessandro Guidi. In this work five symbolic personages—London, the Thames, Fame, the Spirit of Dominion, and the Spirit of Rebellion—were represented by the most renowned singers of the papal choir, led by Fedi; they sang antiphonally with a hundred choristers some declamatory passages which had been set to music by Bernardo Pasquini. On this occasion Corelli directed a formidable orchestra of a hundred and fifty strings.

On the 9th of July, 1687, Corelli was engaged by Cardinal Panfili as his music master at a monthly salary of ten Florentine piastres. He came to live in the Panfili palace in company with Matteo Fornari and his servant, Bernardino Salviati. He was to reside there until 1690: the parish registers bear evidence of this. Moreover, he appeared on the lists of Saint-Louis-des-Français in August, 1689 and in 1690; so one fails to see how, on the death of Christina of Sweden in 1689, he was able to have taken on service at the court of the Duke of Modena, unless it was a stay of short duration. Signor Valdrighi draws attention to the account, dated December 7, 1689, of a confidential agent of the duke at Rome, describing the joy and embarrassment of "Arcangelo dal Violino" on receipt of "a silver casket, admirably chased, and weighing eighty-six ounces, which his Highness has given him as a present." Three years earlier Corelli had refused advantageous terms from the court of Modena so as not to leave Rome, "where he was much esteemed, and payed handsomely." [22]

The accession to the papacy of Alexander VIII (Ottoboni) determined the destiny of Corelli and attached him forever to the Eternal City. One of the first acts of the new pontiff was to nominate his nephew Pietro Ottoboni as Cardinal of San Lorenzo e Damaso and Vice-chancellor of the Church, on November 7, 1689. Pietro Ottoboni was then twenty-six years old. He lived a worldly life—for which he was sometimes bitterly reproached—absorbed in belle-lettres, painting, and the theatre; in 1692 he even staged a *Colombo* of his own composition.[23] But his major passion was music. The dignity with which he was invested by his uncle put immense resources at his disposal, and he made the most liberal use of them. The concerts at the chancellery—a magnificent palace whose salons, library, and museum were famous—soon became the rendezvous of the best Roman society, and the young "porporato" became a most sought after Maecenas, a bestower par excellence of fame and fortune for whomsoever flattered himself on his talent as a virtuoso or composer.

People thronged to the "Mondays" of Ottoboni. Musicians

of stature, for example, Tomaso Albinoni, Mascitti, and Adami da Bolsena, believed they were guaranteeing the success of their works by dedicating them to the young chancellor.

No one was to acquire a place in Ottoboni's favor comparable to that which Arcangelo Corelli held from the outset. The cardinal made him his first violin and director of music, and he was lodged in the palace itself. Ottoboni soon came to treat Corelli not as a salaried servant but as a true friend, whose family was equally dear to him. Ottoboni's letter of March 13, 1700, to the Legate at Ferrara within whose jurisdiction Fusignano lay, was written expressly to commend the brothers of Arcangelo to him; he "beseeches" the Legate to accord his protection "to a family which he [the Cardinal] loves with the most affectionate and special tenderness." In another letter to the same person, he declares himself to be so bound by affection towards Arcangelo "that he no longer distinguishes the passion of his own interest from that of so worthy a subject, and for whose family he can never do enough to make known the tenderness and respect he bears toward them."

Thus lavished with sympathy and admiration, his material well-being largely assured, Corelli was able to devote himself to his art with complete spiritual freedom, and to polish his works at leisure. His music bears the imprint of this leisurely life so different from the rushed and feverish production of his contemporaries, almost all of whom were obliged to furnish one or two operas a season or half a dozen concertos a week. After his arrival at the chancellery, his life was smooth, removed from tumult, without striking vicissitudes. It was but a short time afterward, in 1693, that an *Applauso musicale a quattro voci* [24] (a work recently discovered) made his name prominent, as in 1694 did the trios, Opus IV, dedicated to the cardinal. Indeed, his fame continued to grow: from far off people asked him for lessons. Lord Edgecumbe, one of his aristocratic pupils, commissioned a portrait of Corelli from the English painter Hughes Howard about 1697–1700.

The nephew of Samuel Pepys, in giving an account to his uncle of the midnight mass at the church of San Lorenzo for Christmas, 1699, recorded as noteworthy facts: ". . . Paluccio, an admired young performer, singing, and Corelli, the famous violin, playing in concert with above thirty more, all at the expense of Cardinal Ottoboni, who assisted." [25] In 1700 Corelli was at the head of the instrumental section of the famous *Congregazione dei Musici di Roma sotto l'invocazione di Santa Cecilia.* [26] The same year the publication of his "Opera Quinta," his only set of sonatas for solo violin and bass, sufficed to put him in the very front rank; henceforth by unanimous consent he was esteemed as the greatest composer of instrumental music in the world.

In 1705 and the following years he directed the large orchestras which performed his works on the occasions of the solemn festivities held at the Capitol by the *Accademia del Disegno.*[27] On the 26th of April, 1706, he was received into the *Accademia dei Arcadi,* by far the most exclusive society in Italy, which had reassembled the group of artists and writers of the Palazzo Riario on the death of Christina of Sweden. In what illustrious company did Corelli find himself! Alessandro Scarlatti and Bernardo Pasquini were among the elect.[28] The names attached to them at the time of their admission have been preserved for us, for in this ideal Arcadia each "shepherd" had a double designation—first, a proper name of Grecian derivation, and second, an epithet borrowed from some ancient Arcadian site. Corelli thus became Arcomelo Erimanteo (Arco-melo: leader of singing). Scarlatti and Pasquini were called respectively Terpandro and Protico.

All three had been known to one another for a long time. Pasquini, the singer Fedi, and Corelli, so we are told, were accustomed to meet often, and to keep each other informed of their artistic discoveries. As for Scarlatti, he often directed the concerts at the Palazzo Riario in the heyday of Christina of Sweden.[29] He had arrived in Rome in 1703, and Cardinal Ottoboni, who was his patron also, procured for him the post of assistant chapel master at Santa Maria Maggiore.

In the light of this we are justified in rejecting the date of 1708 assigned by Burney [30] to certain events which associate the two names of Corelli and Scarlatti. It is not irrelevant to note that this English historian has been plagiarized almost word for word by Burgh in his *Anecdotes of Music*, as well as by George Dubourg in his work, *The Violin;* this latter author is a grandson of Matthew Dubourg, one of the best pupils of Geminiani. Here is Burney's account:

A very particular and intelligent friend, upon whose judgment and probity I have most perfect reliance, having had a conversation with Geminiani about five or six years before his death, and a friend of his at that time having had in meditation the writing of a history of Music, he committed to paper, when he got home, the chief particulars of this conversation, supposing they might be of some use to his friend; but as the plan he had in view has been long laid aside, I have been favoured with the anecdotes and particulars that were obtained from Geminiani, which, as they chiefly concern Corelli, and were communicated by one of his most illustrious scholars, who heard and saw what he relates, I shall insert them here.

At the time that Corelli enjoyed the highest reputation, his fame having reached the court of Naples and excited a desire in the King to hear him perform, he was invited by order of His Majesty to that capital. Corelli was at length prevailed on to accept the invitation with some reluctance; but, lest he should not be well accompanied, he took with him his own second violin and violoncello. At Naples he found Alessandro Scarlatti and several other masters; who entreated him to play some of his concertos before the King; this he for some time declined, on account of his whole band not being with him, and there being no time, he said, for a rehearsal. At length, however, he consented and in great fear performed the first of his concertos. His astonishment was very great to find the Neapolitan band executed his concertos almost as accurately at sight as his own band after repeated rehearsals when they had almost got them by heart. 'Si suona,' says he to Matteo [Fornari], his second violin, 'a Napoli.'

After this, being again admitted into his Majesty's presence, and desired to perform one of his sonatas, the King found one of his adagios too long and dry, so that, being tired, he quitted the room to the great mortification of Corelli. Afterwards he was desired to lead in the performance of a masque composed by Scarlatti, which was executed before the King; this he undertook, but from Scarlatti's little knowledge of the violin, the part was somewhat awkward and difficult: in one place it went up to F, and when they came to that passage Corelli failed and was unable to execute it; but he was astonished beyond measure to hear Petrillo, the Neapolitan leader, and the other violins perform that which baffled his skill. A song succeeded this in C-minor, which Corelli led off in C-major; 'Ricominciamo,' said Scarlatti good-naturedly. Still Corelli persisted in the major key till Scarlatti was obliged to call out to him and set him right.

So mortified was poor Corelli with this disgrace and the general bad figure he imagined he had made at Naples, that he stole back to Rome in silence.

The opera supposedly provoking these incidents was, according to Fétis, *Laodicea e Berenice*, where indeed in the third act before the aria "Ti rendo amor la palma," is found a ritornello for violin which extends higher on the E string than Burney says. But far from being crabbedly written, it denotes a perfect familiarity with the instrument:

1.

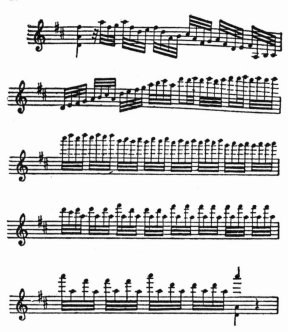

Yet *Laodicea e Berenice* was given at Naples in 1701 and—still according to Fétis—Scarlatti, enlightened by the misadventure of Arcangelo, rewrote the aria in question for the revival of his opera at Rome in 1705. If it is postulated that the journey to Naples took place in 1708,[31] as Professor Edward J. Dent asserts, the perplexity of this latter historian will therefore be shared. Matters turn out better if this journey is assigned to the year 1701, which does not involve any serious objection. Not only does Burney refrain from guaranteeing the date of 1708—"This must have happened about 1708"— but he arrives at the date by relying on the first visit of Scarlatti to Rome in 1709. We have seen earlier, however, that Scarlatti was in Rome on several occasions before his admission into the *Accademia dei Arcadi.*

But it could be that both dates are incorrect. Signor Mario Rinaldi [32] has drawn attention to an entry in the *Diario della Città di Napoli,* which was kept daily by Antonio Bulifon, which reads: "Monday, the 1st of May, 1702: the celebrated violinist Arcangelo Corelli, who is said to be the best in Europe, has arrived in order to play for the opera, which will take place when the singers know their rôles." In point of fact, an opera of Alessandro Scarlatti was performed a week afterwards; but it was not *Laodicea e Berenice,* which was given as early as 1701 as was previously stated. In May, 1702, the work in question was *Tiberio, Imperatore d'Oriente.*

Again it is possible that the anecdote about Corelli may have reference not to an opera but to a serenade, also by Alessandro Scarlatti, which was performed on the 2nd of May and featured as "table music" during the king's evening repast.[33]

As for Petrillo, the hero of this much debated story, Signor Ulisse Prota Giurleo has identified him: [34] his real name was Pietro Marchitelli and he was, in 1702, first violin of the royal chapel and of the theatre of San Bartolomeo.

After the vexatious experience at Naples, if indeed this cascade of misfortunes must be accepted as having occurred, Corelli's existence seems to have regained its customary even tenor. He played regularly each year at the ceremony of Saint Louis until 1709; after that he was mentioned until 1712 in the registers of the parish of San Lorenzo in Damaso as a resident at the chancellery palace along with Matteo Fornari, his right hand.

In 1708 the erroneous news of Corelli's death, circulated in consequence of some sort of confusion,[35] gives us an opportunity to assess the measure of his fame: the Prince Elector Johann Wilhelm von Neuburg-Wittelsbach wrote from Düsseldorf to his agent at Rome, Count Antonio Maria Fede, to tell him his emotion on receipt of the sad news. Fede reassured him (March 3, 1708): "The report which has spread of the death of the famous virtuoso Arcangelo Corelli is absolutely false. For he is living at the court of His Eminence Cardinal Ottoboni, where he constantly gives proofs of his talent, with numerous and celebrated professors whom the generosity of so worthy a prelate maintains." The same Count Fede, at the instigation of the Prince Elector, asked Cardinal Ottoboni to induce Corelli to compose a work expressly dedicated to Johann Wilhelm. In the month of May, 1708, Corelli handed over to the Prince a "Concertino da Camera" which was later to figure among the four chamber concertos of Opus VI, dedicated to the said Prince Elector. Dr. Alfred Einstein, to whom we owe these details, published the covering letter, which is of quite conventional obeisance, and to which Johann Wilhelm replied with much good will.

In this year of 1708 there occurred another well-known incident, the report of which, it seems, was first propagated

by John Mainwaring.[36] Corelli, as first violin, was directing
the orchestra in Rome for the overture of the *Triumph of
Time* by Handel in the presence of the composer, who attempted to impose on Corelli his own style of playing which
was appreciably more impetuous and accentuated. Our violinist not succeeding in this, Handel, in his impatience, snatched
the instrument from him and began to play in his stead. To
which Corelli simply retorted, "But, my dear Saxon, this music
is in the French style which I do not understand." ("Ma, caro
Sassone, questa musica è nel stilo francese, di ch'io non
m'intendo!") We shall see when we analyze Corelli's technique
that this incident does not run counter to probability any more
than does the incident at Naples.

Perhaps it was in order to efface an unpleasant memory and
to render discreet homage to Corelli that Handel in his oratorio, *La Resurrezione,* performed the same year in Rome, gave
one character an air to sing through which loomed the already
celebrated gavotte of Opus V: [37]

2.

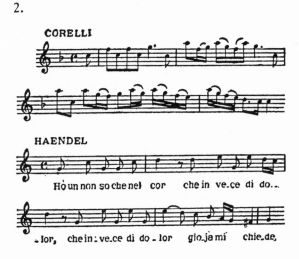

About the same time Giuseppe Valenti dedicated to the master a sonata entitled *La Corelli*,[38] in the style of French pieces for the viol or harpsichord. This tends to raise doubts as to the rivalry which, according to Geminiani (Burney, III, 553), existed between them. Geminiani states that Valenti's success, and that of an oboe player whose name is lost grievously affected Corelli and engendered a melancholia which was to hasten his end.

In point of fact, all we know is that Corelli ceased to appear in public after the beginning of 1710, and that at the very end of 1712, being ill, he had himself borne to his chamber in the Palazotto Ermini. He had rented this lodging, comprised of three rooms and kitchen, at the time he became a resident in the sumptuous palace of Cardinal Ottoboni in order that he might store there his personal belongings and especially his paintings. Normally the apartment was occupied by his brother Giacinto and his nephew Arcangelo.

Feeling very ill on the 5th of January, 1713, he drew up his last will which he handed over, duly sealed, to his usual confessor, Dom Pier Paolo Sala, a Theatine of the monastery of San Andrea della Valle.

He died during the night of the 8th of January. His brother and his nephew were not in Rome, and the news was dispatched to them at Faenza by Girolam Sorboli, one of the executors of the will. The nephew Arcangelo in turn communicated the news to his uncle Vincenzo Mascarini di Massalombarda in a lengthy letter, which Dr. Piancastelli has printed. It says, among other things, that the deceased "has passed into the other life in a pure and angelic interior state, and that his death has downcast Rome and the World"; that "Cardinal

Ottoboni has expressed his affliction by a letter of condolence written in his own hand, wherein he gives an assurance that his protection will not cease and that, wishing to show the World in what esteem he held my uncle, he has had him embalmed and placed in a triple bier of lead, cypress, and chestnut wood, and laid in a tomb of marble with an epitaph which the same Sr. Cardinal has had constructed in the church of the Rotunda, all at his own expense."

So then Corelli was buried through the good offices of Cardinal Ottoboni in the church of Santa Maria della Rotunda—the Pantheon—where his tomb is to be found in the chapel of Saint Joseph to the left of the entrance. Regarding this interment in the Pantheon, Dr. Piancastelli points out that in 1713 it had not the connotation of national homage which was attached to such burial at a later date after Antonio Canova had had the idea of assembling in the Rotunda statues of illustrious Italians of all times. However, the chapel of Saint Joseph, since the 16th century, had been the specific resting place of painters, architects, and sculptors who belonged to the *Artistica Congregazione dei Virtuosi al Pantheon*. In order that the burial of Corelli might be allowed there, for he was a musician and a stranger to the parish, a special enactment instigated by Cardinal Ottoboni was necessary: "ex concessione," says the funeral deed, and the inscription engraved on the tombstone intimates a pontifical indulgence—"indulgente Clemente XI P."

An anonymous bust, attributed to Angelo Rossi, embellished the tomb at the Pantheon. In 1820 the sculpture was transported to the gallery of the Capitol where Cardinal Consalvi had gathered together the busts of famous Italians. Beneath was the following epitaph, which has survived:

D. O. M.

ARCANGELO CORELLIO E FUSIGNANO
PHILIPPI WILLELMI COMITIS PALATINI RHENI
S. R. I. PRINCIPIS AC ELECTORIS
Beneficentia
Marchioni de Ladensburg
quod eximiis animi dotibus
et incomparabili in musicis modulis peritia
summis pontificibus apprima carus
italiæ atque exteris nationibus admirationi fuerit
indulgente CLEMENTE XI P. O. M.
PETRUS CARDINALIS OTTHOBONUS S. R. E. VIC. CAN.
ET GALLIARUM PROTECTOR
Liiristi celeberrimo
inter familiares suos iam diu adscito
eius nomen immortalitati commendaturus
M. P. C.
Vixit annos LIX mens. X Dies XX
Obiit VI id. Januarii Annos Sal. MDCCXIII *

This inscription, except for four lines, reproduces the epitaph which appears on the frontispiece of Corelli's Opus VI
which was completed shortly before the composer's death,
although its publication did not take place until the end of
1714. The difference concerns the phrase which relates to
the ennoblement of Corelli, which appears only on the memo-

* To God the best and greatest. Pietro, Cardinal Ottoboni, Vice-Chancellor
of the Holy Roman Church and Protector of France, with the permission of
Clement XI, best and worthiest of pontiffs, directed the founding of this
monument to Arcangelo Corelli of Fusignano, Marquis of Ladensburg
through the kindness of Philipp Wilhelm, Count Palatine of the Rhine,
Prince and Elector of the Holy Roman Empire. For his excellent qualities of
mind and incomparable skill in musical rhythms he was eminently dear to the
supreme pontiffs, the celebrated lyrist being long since acknowledged among
the members of the Cardinal's household. He lived 59 years, 10 months, and
20 days, dying on the 8th of January in the year of salvation 1713.

rial stone. It must be that this was added after the event and subsequent to August 10, 1715. For on this date the marquisate of Landenburg was conferred on Ippolito Corelli, his elder brother, by the Prince Elector Johann Wilhelm on the entreaties of Cardinal Ottoboni, as always, and in consideration "of the declared and special protection" which he exercised over the Corelli family.[39] It may be noted that after 1706 another brother of Arcangelo, Giacinto, had the title of "Nobile del Sacro Imperio Romano." The patent of nobility, dated the 4th of December, 1705, is at present in the possession of the Marchese Vittorio Emmanuele Corelli in Rome.[40]

It is not true that in exchange for such friendship Corelli considered himself obliged to appoint his benefactor, who was already overloaded with fortune, as his sole legatee.

According to Burney, Hawkins, and their plagiarists, his estate consisted of a capital of about six thousand pounds and a precious collection of paintings bequeathed in entirety to Cardinal Ottoboni, who was supposed to have generously relinquished the capital for the family of the deceased and only retained the paintings.

Here again the recent researches of Dr. Piancastelli and Alberto Cametti have established the truth. Thanks to them we have the actual text of the will as well as the inventory which was drawn up immediately after Corelli's death. The will, now in the state archives in Rome, reads thus:

To Sr. Cardinal Ottoboni, my patron, I bequeath a picture of his own choosing, and I beg him to have me interred wheresoever seems fitting to him. To Sr. Matteo Fornari I leave all my violins and all my manuscripts, also the plates of my Fourth Work, and in addition the Sixth Work, the profit from which, if there is any, shall be for him. To the Eminence Cardinal Colonna I leave a picture on canvas by Breughel. To Pippo, my manservant, I bequeath a half doubloon a month and to his sister Olimpia four testers a month, during their lifetime.

I nominate my brothers as residuary legatees. The executors of my will are to be Sr. D. Giuseppe Mondini and Sr. Girolamo Sorboli, who will arrange my obsequies and have five hundred masses held for me. Given the 5th day of January 1713.

I, Arcangelo Corelli, by my own hand.

Pippo, the manservant, or to give him his true name, Filippo Graziani, lived in the apartment at the Palazzetto Ermini where Giacinto and the nephew Arcangelo usually resided; he probably supervised the maintenance of their personal effects and the collection of paintings. Giuseppe Mondini was a maker of harpsichords, reputedly in the Piazza Navone.[41]

The apartment, according to the inventory drawn up after Corelli's death, contained one hundred and thirty-six pictures or drawings, of which twenty-two were by Trevisani, two by Maratta, and three by Cignani—all personal friends of Corelli. Trevisani, like Corelli, had been granted an allowance and accommodation by Cardinal Ottoboni. Among the valuable canvases were several by Trevisani, the Breughel bequeathed to Cardinal Colonna, landscapes by Poussin, and a madonna by Sassoferrato. The furnishing was not especially luxurious; in the entrance hall some chairs and stools in red damask or in leather, and four tables, including one for writing; in the gallery, the door of which was decorated by a leather hanging, four large stools and two armchairs covered in red calfskin, and a table of oriental alabaster supported by a siren in gilt wood; in the bed chamber a simple bed without a canopy, a *prie-dieu* with crucifix of burnished brass, two chests of drawers, a writing desk, and seven seats. One of the chests contained 71 shares in the Mont-de-Piété, to the value of 7100 écus in all. A letter of the 22nd of April, 1702, addressed by Arcangelo to his brother Ippolito, informs us that he then possessed 57 of these shares.[42] Added to this some silverware and clothes. As for musical instruments, the inventory makes mention of a two-manual harpsichord with carved gilt feet and a cover (case) of leather with gilt flowers, an old violoncello, two violins, one of them a mediocre instrument, and a "violone" (a double bass viol) in its case. Unfortunately not one of these instruments has been preserved: it may be Corelli's harpsichord that we find mentioned among the effects left by Fornari to his nephew Matteo in 1722, and by the nephew to *his* beneficiaries in 1761, described as being "un cimbalo a due registri con cassa levatora con suoi piedi torniti all'antica e dorati con sua coperti di corame."

As for the violins, Choron and Fayolle tell us that one of them was given by Giardini before his departure for Russia in 1796 to an amateur of Como by the name of Ciceri.[43] This account is confirmed by Gerber, according to whom the English virtuoso William Corbett brought one of Corelli's violins (perhaps the one he is said to have given to Fornari?) to London soon after the death of the master. This violin, dated 1578 and boasting a case painted by Annibal Carracci, remained for some time in the hands of a gentleman of Newcastle on whose death Avison acquired it so that it might be offered to Giardini. Ciceri still had it in his possession in 1825: it is not known what happened to it after that. The article devoted to Johann Peter Salomon, the friend of Haydn, in Grove's *Dictionary of Music*

(IV, 514) attributes to him the ownership of a Stradivarius which is supposed to have borne the name of Corelli, its old owner, and which, it is claimed, passed on the death of Salomon in 1815 into the hands of one of his friends. All trace of this instrument has also vanished.

A steadfast calm is the trait of character which Corelli's biographers most complacently stress. It may be that his Christian name, with its angelic connotation, and perhaps too the tales of Geminiani as recounted by Burney, are responsible for this reputation for benignity. It is scarcely credible that it was never belied. The very animated portrait painted by Howard about 1700 indicates anything but a smiling passivity. There is no softness in Corelli's attitude; large eyes, by no means deep-set, peer into the distance, but not into vacuity; the curve of his lip is resolute; all the features of his face seem to denote decision.

In the fervor of performance the customary placidity of the master gave way to an outburst of feeling which might create rather considerable surprise today. "A person who heard him perform says that whilst he was playing on the violin it was usual for his countenance to be distorted, his eyes to become as red as fire and his eyeballs to roll as in an agony" (Hawkins, II, 674). Supposing the picture to be true, let us remember before reacting with astonishment that the demands of the public with regard to virtuosi have somewhat changed in two centuries. At this period, especially in Italy, the sober gestures of a Thibaud or a Heifetz might have been thought offensive. According to a Frenchman living in 1700, the Italian sonatas "fill the senses, the imagination, and the soul with such vehemence that players of the violin who perform such works cannot stay themselves from being transported by them, and caught up in their frenzy; they torture their violins and their bodies so that they act like men possessed." [44] Locatelli, in 1741, "plays with so much fire that he must use up a few dozen violins a year." [45] Even in France where players were less demonstrative, Corrette begged the accompanist to conduct himself with particular discretion in the cadences *a tasto solo* in order not to restrain the spirit of the violinist "when he is in his *enthusiasm*," that is to say, in that state of exaltation to which, we are assured, the placid Corelli let himself be carried away.

A simple discussion of theory could also, on occasion, exacerbate him. We have an example of this in the curious episode called "the fifths." [46] Among the heroes of this affair was one of the luminaries of the Bologna School, Giovan Paolo Colonna, master of the chapel of San Petronio, a charter member and several times president of the *Accademia dei Filarmonici*, and a prolific and esteemed composer. At his house musical gatherings were held during which the performance of works alternated with aesthetic discussions to which they might give rise. His pupils and the principal virtuosi of Bologna were habitués of these gatherings.

Toward the middle of 1685, an important local publisher, Monti, published Corelli's Opus II trios, which had been previously brought out in Rome. This publication created a wave of lively curiosity among Corelli's former fellow citizens, and Colonna arranged a reading of the new work at one of the first meetings following its issue. When the players had arrived at a certain passage of the third trio, as Colonna himself reported, they "began to look askance at one another: when I asked them what was the matter they beat about the bush (*storce-*

vano) and declined to pass judgment as the work was by a master and they were novices; I enjoined them to speak all the same, and one of them replied that it seemed to him that the work 'was full of fifths'." Colonna assured them that the composer had certainly written with a knowledge of what he was doing, and that the fifths could not be erroneous. The sight reading was then continued to the end, and the trio applauded. But the pupils took up the discussion once more at the close of the session, so that Colonna, to close the matter, delegated his friend Matteo Zani to ask Corelli personally to explain the few controversial bars.

To Zani's very deferential and circumspect letter came an intransigent and impatient reply dated Rome, October 17, 1685: "I received in your very polished letter the sheet which contained the passage from the sonata where these virtuosi found themselves in difficulty. I am not at all astonished thereby, and in the light of this, I understand very well the range of their science, which scarcely goes beyond the first principles of composition and of modulation; since if they had advanced further in the art and were acquainted with its finesse and profundity, and knew what harmony is and how it can charm and sustain the human spirit, they would not have had such scruples, which normally are born of ignorance. With an exact and long assiduity and a practice derived from the best teachers in Rome, I have endeavored to make their examples my own, knowing full well that all work must be grounded on reason and on the pattern of the most excellent teachers. . . ." He added that "to satisfy the curiosity of these young gentlemen," he was going to try and make himself clear to them. And he explained that he himself had figured the consecutive fifths above the bass to throw his intention into relief, and to prove there was neither negligence nor chance at this stage. If, he went on to say, instead of a quarter-note rest he had dotted the preceding note, which would not have altered the note-values, even beginners would not have been upset for nothing. But he had chosen this notation in order

3.

that the quarter-notes of the bass might be detached and played *smorzando*. It may be noted that Corelli's explanation is that which G. Gaspari offers in his version in *La Musica in Bologna*

(p. 15): "The discussion is recorded in manuscript in the Liceo Musicale di Bologna; but it is singular that in this polemic we do not see the true reason advanced for which this disputed passage is sound, namely, that the rests in the bass are tantamount to tied notes." (See Example 3, page 49.) Corelli added several contemptuous observations "for those who are in the dark [in obscuris]," and claimed for himself authority from the unreserved approbation of colleagues such as Francesco Foggia, Antimo Liberati, and Matteo Simonelli.

The letter provoked a great stir in Bologna. Through Zani's agency, it actually reached Colonna who, "confounded" by a reply "in such degree bitter and obnoxious," sought the help of his old colleague Antimo Liberati.

We do not propose to follow the development of the quarrel in which G. B. Vitali, Celani, and Giacomo Antonio Perti were successively involved. The victory was bound to go to Corelli and, in his person, to the Roman School. For it is quite probable—the opinion is that of Francesco Vatielli—that the irritation of the Bolognese and the resistance of the Romans were due to the fact that the former viewed with rancor the slipping away from them of a master from whom they had anticipated great renown for their city, and the latter were resolved to defend the artistic reputation of so precious a recruit.

What interests us most in this incident is the violence of our hero, who is commonly represented as a little stained glass saint. This angry conduct, it is true, can be construed in praise of Corelli, who was not ungrateful toward Bologna, which had nurtured him, but who was indignant at an obsolete pedantry and who had a just consciousness of his worth; traits so much more acceptable in that "they destroy that conventional and honeymouthed image which had been formed of him in the text books" (Piancastelli). Let us note, by the way, an unexpected consequence of this controversy over the fifths. Beyond doubt it lies at the root of the rumor which was bound to gain some measure of ground, namely, that "Corelli was indebted to another composer for the bass part of his compositions"—against which the English theorist Avison made protest as late as 1775.

There is also to be taken into account a jocular Corelli, one who once made a pun on his Christian name, which pleasantry has remained well known. The German virtuoso Nicolas Adam Strungk having just arrived in Rome in the entourage of Ernst August of Hanover, he chanced to find himself one day in the presence of Corelli, who asked him if he were a musician. He replied that he played the harpsichord: at which Corelli, in order to be agreeable, offered to accompany him on his violin. Thus it was. Then Corelli inquired whether he played the violin at all, seeing he had such a mastery of the keyboard. "A little," replied the German. He began, and as Corelli was commending him on his bowing and saying how regrettable it seemed that he had not devoted more time to the violin, Strungk started to play the instrument with a *scordatura* tuning (we know that Walther, Biber, and all the Austro-German School at that time used this abnormal tuning which facilitated polyphonic playing), to the great astonishment of Corelli, who exclaimed: "Sir, here they call me Archangel; but they ought to call you Archdevil!" [47]

We know too that Corelli was simple in his tastes, as the inventory of his furniture and clothes testifies. Whenever Handel used to speak of him, it is claimed that he deliberately avoided any encomiums, which gives a sarcastic tone to his utterances: "His two dominant characteristics were his admiration of pictures, which they say he never paid for, and an extreme parsimony. His wardrobe was not extensive. Ordinarily he went about clothed in black, and he used to wear a dark cloak; he was always on foot, and protested vigorously if one tried to make him take a carriage." But Hawkins affirms that Handel harbored no captious reservations, and that his remarks were without malevolence.[48]

Did Corelli have the accommodating disposition of a courtier or not? One should not hasten to judge him by his dedicatory prefaces, all of them addressed to advantageous patrons with a good deal of modesty: "To the luminous reflection of the royal crown of Your Majesty, these feeble and humble musical effusions have recourse in order to obtain some illumination. . . ." (To Christina of Sweden, dedicatory inscription of Opus I.) "The beautiful soul, the great soul of Your Electoral Highness, so finely fashioned by heaven, and endowed to be the examplar and ideal of the perfect heroine, possesses the distinguished merit of such complete harmony that it could not fail to unite to a concert of so many virtues a sweet inclination for music: from whence it follows that Your Electoral Highness, approaching this art seriously and not as a simple divertisement has a sound and scientific knowledge of it. All those of my profession ought then to be proud of the honor which Your Electoral Highness does them. . . ." (To Sophia Charlotte of Brandenburg, dedicatory inscription of Opus V.)

This language is that of all dedications of the time. There is a sort of established formulary, a code of outbidding, which all composers throughout Europe practiced, and which by reason of its universality no more compromised its authors than it flattered its dedicatees.

Corelli had his chosen *milieux*, it is true; he lived among cardinals and the highest Roman dignitaries. But while his official residence was with them at the chancellery, or at the Panfili palace, it may be conjectured that his predilection was for the little town apartment with the paintings by his friends Maratta, Cignani, and Trevisani,[49] his harpsichord, his violins, and the writing desk with its drawers full of manuscripts.

Music, painting, and friendship seem to have sufficed to grace his life. Although the Abbé Laurenti invented the admirable match with a good dowry that was allegedly offered to the young master in France, this powerful romancer does not go so far as to round off the marriage; "the firm intent of Corelli being to live celibate since he felt no other passion than music within himself." [50]

The little we know does justify us, however, in conjuring up for ourselves a coherent enough picture of him; of a man of gentle nature, less timid than reserved, at times capable of raising his voice, simple in his manners, sometimes jocular, firm in friendship, passionate toward his art, and unable to compromise with the respect he bore for it, as an examination of his work will show.

II

Corelli's Work

THE TRIOS, OPUS I TO IV

CORELLI'S FAME rests entirely on six books of instrumental music. The bibliography at the end of this book does, indeed, contain a certain number of other works in manuscript or print which with more or less probability are attributed to Corelli. But in a manner of speaking, there is hardly a trace of vocal music to be found among these; nothing of secular music; and two manuscripts of religious music, the authenticity of which is not established. (See Musical Bibliography, page 206.)

This abstention, odd in an era when it was customary to tackle all genres, and coupled, furthermore, with the slow spacing of six books over a span of thirty years, tellingly conveys the scruples of the composer. In contrast to Vitali, Albinoni, and Bassani—who have to their credit as many masses, cantatas, and even operas, as sonatas—he writes little, publishes still less, and limits the study of his entire lifetime to the repertoire of bowed instruments.

Analysis of his works is greatly assisted by the fact that their order of appearance coincides with their grouping by genres; the first four collections are solely composed of trios; the fifth is the famous book of sonatas for solo violin and bass, which was the pivot, so to speak, for the aesthetic controversies in which French and Italians passionately engaged for a quarter of a century; the sixth, finally, contains the concerti grossi.

Corelli began by giving to the public four books of *Sonate a tre* which appeared respectively in 1681, 1685, 1689, and 1694. This writing was an act of complete submission to prevailing fashions. For reasons which can only be conjectured, the Italian masters had evinced a singular predilection for the combination of two violins and bass since the origin of the sonata form at the beginning of the 18th century.

It might have seemed natural for the first attempts at ensemble instrumental music to be planned on the model of the old vocal polyphony. The string quartet thus replaced, without jarring, the hierarchy of voices of soprano, alto, tenor, and bass; and about 1600 we find Florentio Maschera, Adriano Banchieri, and Giovanni Gabrieli writing canzoni and sinfonie for quartet or double quartet in a style directly inspired by the old *a cappella* choirs. But this survival was without roots; and the Italian genius was to devote itself to ousting the polyphonic complexity on behalf of a more expansive style with more independent melodic contours, and less closely subordinated to the exigencies of counterpoint. It was, at an interval of some years, the evolution which had begun to realize itself in dramatic music and to follow a parallel course; it was the same search for expression, which was being contrasted with the alleged aridity of the art of the previous century, an art henceforth regarded as pedantic and of an outmoded scholasticism.

The surprising thing was that these revolutionaries, however lucid their monodic ideal might be, seemed disconcerted at the thought of making it prevail; the sonata for solo instrument, with or without a figured bass, remained a rarity for almost the whole of the 17th century. Until 1670 only rare examples of it are to be found in the works of Biagio Marini, Giovanni Battista Fontana, Martino Pesenti, Uccellini, and a few others; most composers halted at the midpoint, the trio sonata balanced, like the vocal canzoni of the preceding century, for two sopranos and bass. Ecorcheville has tried to explain this:

The reasons for this predilection are the same as those for the evolution of Italian music. The Italian trio may be considered both as the first complication of sheer simple melody and the last striving for the simplification of polyphony; it is the point of contact of these two counter movements. The Italians halted there because it was the easiest form to handle and also did not lose all the advantages of polyphony. They turned it to the fullest possible account, thanks to a very adroit disposition of voices, which consisted of entrusting two of these voices— the principal ones—to two violins and the other to a violoncello alone or reinforced by a harpsichord, which formed the bass. The absence of an intermediate part, and the space of nearly two octaves between the two soprano voices and the bass thus obviated all chiaroscuro, all diffused shading; the melodic strands of the violini soared high above the low register of the violone or of the cembalo and stood out in full light. And, moreover, the melodic element was not a single line as in some artless accompanied song or some unpretentious dance air. The double design of the two violins intertwined in diverting arabesques evolved according to the laws of counterpoint, and gave to the work that character of conscientious craftsmanship which was expected in a sonata. [51]

It would seem advisable to maintain some reservations on "the character of conscientious craftsmanship," which the public perhaps did not expect at the dawn of instrumental music as they do today, after a century and a half of the Conservatoire and fifty years of the Schola Cantorum, to speak only of France, have given the sonata form a formidable gravity. The "absence of an intermediate part" is also a slight inexactitude. An intermediary contrapuntal voice is in fact lacking in this scoring: but as often as not it was furnished by the harpsichord, organ, lute, or chitarrone which realized the figured bass; and under the fingers of an expert musician this realization could be richer, even melodically, than the instrumental tenor voice which the trio had renounced. The theorists of the time tell us that the accompanist, far from being merely content to strike and hold chords, must adapt his style to that of the ensemble, "le commune ed ordinarie maniere del sinfoneggiare" (Doni, *Compendio del Trattato di generi e di modi*, 1635).

Without refuting the explanation of Ecorcheville, a mark of defiance or timidity in respect to individual lyricism is discernible in the long fidelity of the Italians to the trio sonata. In the same way the concerto for soloist only dares to make its way after a long experience of the concerto grosso, where virtuosity remained collective; and Vivaldi, the first in this matter, had the temerity to present in the *adagio* a true counterpart of the operatic aria, exposing the virtuoso to the concentrated attention of his audience and forcing him to express his own personality in the same way a singer must at the climax of an opera.

Such was not Corelli's ambition, at least at the outset of his career. He found numerous and varied prototypes of a firmly established genre with his teachers, and especially with that

Bolognese school whose influence Vatielli has so clearly delineated: [52] in the works of Maurizio Cazzati, of G. B. Vitali, of Torelli, and of Pietro degli Antonii, collections of trio sonatas predominate. Corelli harked back to them and, as R. Giazotto (*Tomaso Albinoni*, p. 71) has justly observed, the insistence with which throughout his first four sets he confined himself within the trio sonata form "denotes the full conviction of the composer, who affirms his faith in a structure and instrumental disposition which is absolutely determinate as to architectonic equilibrium and density of sonorities."

Like his predecessors, Corelli adopted a layout in four parts, engraved in four separate folios, which at first seems inconsistent with the title of trios: two violins, a bowed bass instrument (violoncello or violone) or an archlute, plus an instrument assigned to realizing the figured bass: the organ for the church sonatas, the harpsichord for the chamber sonatas.

Corelli also maintained the distinction, by then traditional, between sonatas *da chiesa* and sonatas *da camera*, which latter works the catalogues of Estienne Roger of Amsterdam in 1700 listed as *Baletti*.

Without recounting the historical development of the sonata at this point, for which one can profitably have recourse to the first chapter of the masterly work of L. de la Laurencie,[53] I shall confine myself to recalling the distinction which Canon de Brossard, a contemporary of Corelli, established between the two genres:

> There are sonatas, so to speak, in infinite styles, but the Italians generally reduce them to two types.
> The first type comprises the sonatas *da Chiesa*, that is to say proper to the Church, which usually begin with a grave and

majestic movement appropriate to the dignity and sanctity of the place; after which some gay and animated Fugue is taken up. These are the ones which are properly known as *Sonates*.

The second type comprises the *Sonates* called *da Camera*, that is to say, proper to the chamber. To be more exact, these are suites of several short pieces apt for dancing [more correctly, derived from old dances], and composed in the same Mode or Key. These sorts of sonatas generally begin with a *Prélude*, or *petite Sonate*, which serves as a preparation for all the other movements; afterwards come the *Allemande*, the *Pavane*, the *Courante*, and other dances or serious airs; then follow the *Gigues*, the *Passacailles*, the *Gavottes*, the *Menuets*, the *Chaconnes*, and other lively Airs, and all that composed in the same Key or Mode and played in sequence, forms a Sonata *da Camera*.[54]

Corelli observed the distinction by grouping in Opera I and III the church trios and excluding the chamber trios, which he assembled in Opera II and IV. The mere wording of the titles attests the greater seriousness with which he considered the church type: for these he indicated as instruments two violins and bass "plus" organ, while he prescribed for the chamber trios two violins and a violone "or" a harpsichord.

The texture of the church trios is, in Corelli's conception, richer and more elaborate, which even a superficial glance at the text will confirm at once. In the trios of Opus II and Opus IV the bass part for the bowed instrument or the archlute is an exact repetition of the figured bass. This is not true in Opus I and Opus III. Again and again the bowed bass instrument is entrusted with much more rapid figures than the figured bass (finale of the 2nd sonata, Opus I): whereas the figured bass pursues its uniform course, the bowed bass instrument is halted in order with more arresting eloquence to resume with a fugal design analogous to that of the violins. In the same Opus I the *vivace* of the 4th sonata and the first *allegro* of the 7th are equally characteristic. The differences are less marked in Opus III, but appreciable instances are to be found in the *allegros* of the 1st and 5th sonatas, and the *vivace* of the 12th.

Yet it should be noted in passing that the bass players of the chamber sonatas were not to refrain from improvising harmonic lines suggested to them by the figuring of the continuo; and the richness of the harmony depended solely on their ingenuity: they were practically forced to do this when the harpsichord was lacking. It cannot be repeated often enough (we shall return to this point apropos Opus V) that the musical texts of this period, and particularly those of the Italian masters, are far from possessing the categorical imperativeness of a modern score: they transmit suggestions to the interpreter, rather than orders.

The church sonata leaves less latitude to individual fancy, out of respect for the sacred edifice whose majesty would be affronted by inappropriate embroideries: on this point it has even been written that Rome had forbidden instrumental ensembles in church until the unanimous admiration engendered by the trios of Corelli undermined the ruling.[55] Furthermore, the composer was at pains, in expressly writing out the part for the bass stringed instrument, to leave the least possible to the discretion of the performer: he knew that compositions of a type considered the touchstone of real talent would be examined with a particularly critical eye.

Most assuredly the difference existing between the chamber

trios and the church trios of Corelli is not so marked as terminology would lead one to suppose. Riehl writes, not without point: "Bach has, in more than one Sarabande of his Suites or Partitas, introduced the ecclesiastical style into the music of the dance. Reversely Corelli introduces the forms of the dance into music for the church." Indeed, in Opus I alone, the *allegro* in triple meter of the 1st trio, the second *allegro* of the 3rd, and the *vivace* of the 8th recall the minuet, just as the *allegros* of the 4th and the 8th bring to mind the allemande; and the finales of the 2nd, 5th, 6th, and 7th the gigue. The corrente is suggested by the finale of the 9th, and likewise the gavotte by the *presto* of the 4th.

In a general way—the observation is made by Professor Bukofzer (*Music in the Baroque Era*, p. 233)—"The two last movements both depend on the dance; the third movement is usually a broad and chordal *adagio* cantilena in the stylized triple time of the saraband, the last one a lively gigue. This inclusion of dance patterns in the church sonata marks the beginning of the internal disintegration of the form which coincides in the works of Corelli with its external stabilization in four stereotyped movements. The chamber sonatas (with harpsichord continuo) open with a prelude in strict style, which in turn betrays the influence of the church sonata, and then present two or three dances written in continuo-homophony but not without slight contrapuntal touches."

Nevertheless a certain number of permanent characteristics distinguish the two genres. Without discussing further the instrumental layout, of which we have spoken earlier, we will look at the terminology used by Corelli to designate movements.

However, forbidding statistics may look in tabular presentation, they do have the merit of clarity. Here, then, is a recapitulation of the movements of the various trios:

MOVEMENTS	CHURCH TRIOS		CHAMBER TRIOS	
	OPUS I	OPUS III	OPUS II	OPUS IV
Grave	11	9	1	2
Largo	3	6		
Adagio	10	7	2	1
Andante		1		
Allegro	20	22		
Vivace	3	7		
Presto	1	1		
Preludio			8	12
Allemanda			12	7
Corrente			5	8
Sarabanda			4	3
Gavotta			3	4
Giga			6	4
Ciacona			1	

The chaconne, *ciacona*, constitutes by itself the 12th trio of Opus 11, just as the *follia* is the 12th sonata of Opus V.

The presence of but one *andante* in the four sets of trios will be noted in contrast to the *andante* frequency which prevails from the advent of the great classics; although the *grave* and the *adagio* are a constant feature of these works of Corelli, and even the chamber trio sometimes adopts them in place of the sarabanda.

With regard to the number of movements, the Corellian church trio differs slightly from the chamber trio, and quite differently from the way one might expect, since the latter derives from the ancient suite of dances which easily subdivides into five, six, or seven sections, if not more. But it is the church trio which generally is in four movements or more, and the chamber trio which tends to be restricted to three.

If we designate slow movements by *S* and fast movements by *F*, we find in Opus I ten trios, each with four movements, thus:

6 of the type *S F S F*
3 of the type *F S S F*
1 of the type *F S F F*

while one trio—the 10th, in which Professor Bukofzer discerns a return to the technique of the old variation canzona—is in five movements, *S F F S F* and one (the 7th) in three movements, *F S F*.

In Opus III, ten trios are in four movements:

7 of the type *S F S F*
1 of the type *S F F F*
1 of the type *F S F F*
1 of the type *F F S F*

One (the 5th) is in five movements, *S S F S F;* and one (the 12th) is in nine movements, *S F F S F F S F F*. We should add that a number of these so-called slow movements are mere episodes of a few measures, either introductory or transitional, so that in actual fact the scheme contracts to four movements.

It cannot be claimed, furthermore, that Corelli made innovations in one way or another: the majority of his predecessors—among them those who had published their works at Bologna—employed this division of the sonata into four movements, which division is to be found very frequently in the works of Giovanni Battista Vitali in his collections of 1669 and 1671.[56] But such an arrangement was not obligatory. The Italians did not hesitate to write sonatas in five or six movements, and as late as 1682 the German Westhoff published one which involved no less than ten indications of tempo and nine separate movements: *Adagio con una dolce Maniera, Allegro, Adagio, Allegro overo un poco presto, Adagio, Aria adagio assai. La guerra [allegro], Aria tutto adagio, Vivace* (C), *Vivace* (6/4).

In this connection it is important to remember that liberties which would be hardly imaginable for a musician today were enjoyed by performers vis-à-vis musical texts almost to the end of the eighteenth century: not only could they embellish the melodic line as they wished, modify the orchestration, and give body to the harmonies, but they could even play only the movements of their choice in a sonata or a suite. In the *Avertissement* of his *Sonate Accademiche* of 1744, Veracini declares: "If each of these sonatas comprises four or five movements, remember that this has been done for the sake of the richness and enhancement of the book, and in order to give the greatest diversion to lovers and dilettanti of music. But two or three movements of each of these sonatas, chosen according to your tastes, would be enough to make a sonata of true proportions."

Among the chamber trios, four out of eleven of those of Opus II (not taking the chaconne into account) are in three movements; six are in four movements, and one is in five movements, including a short *grave* of four measures. Opus IV includes seven trios of three movements each, and five of four movements. In Opus II eight trios begin with a slow *preludio*, and three with a slow *allemanda*. All the trios of Opus IV commence with a slow *preludio*. All the chamber trios end with a lively dance: *giga, tempo di gavotta, allemanda, allegro,* or *corrente allegro,* and once (Opus IV, No. 8) by a *sarabanda allegro*.

In the four sets Corelli observed complete tonal unity: out of 48 trios, 29 have all their movements in the same key; the other 19 allow a slow movement in the relative minor. Yet the majority of these *adagio, grave,* or *largo* movements which open in the relative key do not stay in it, but cadence appropriately for ending in the principal key.

Corelli showed himself rather bolder in the choice of keys. He preferably employed those aligned with the open strings, but sometimes he ventured to write in *c, f,* and *f*-sharp.

CONSTRUCTION

When the construction of each movement in particular is studied—this is as relevant for the four books of trios as for the sonatas for violin and bass of Opus V—one confronts a variety of types, or, rather, a disconcerting instability. This occurs because the sonata form was far from having been fixed, and did not yet impose on the composer the onerous constraints against which, at long intervals, creative temperaments would have to strive. In a work which is directed at the general reader we shall not study all the patterns worked out by Corelli, but only the principal ones, which, in point of fact, embrace numerous intermediary types.

In a general way the pieces contrapuntally conceived, written in a continuous texture without repeats, can be

distinguished primarily from pieces more or less homophonic
—this term being used, for want of a better, as the antithesis
of polyphonic—with repeats.

The majority of movements of the church trios and a few
preludes and slow movements of the chamber trios belong
to the first category; but once again there is no absolutely
clear demarcation line between the two genres.[57]

In this first category are two distinct types. One is that
with the initial *grave*. Nearly always this type begins with the
exposition of a rather short theme of two to eight or ten
measures which extends by sequences of much less definite
melodic significance. To this development, or, rather, to this
extenuation, neither amplitude nor textual repetition of theme
nor compartmentation by repeats is necessary: as in the old
motet, of which the church trio bears trace, the interplay
of imitations and syncopations is an end in itself. Here is a
characteristic example of this style of writing taken from
the first trio of Opus I:

4.

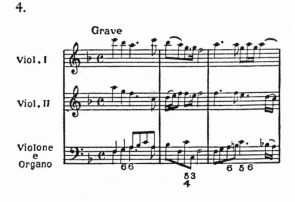

The second type of movement with sustained development is the fugue, the principal element of the church trios.

This, by far the most "written" movement, is tantamount in importance to the *allegro* of the classical sonata. In Corelli's work it is almost invariably the second movement, an *allegro* or *vivace;* occasionally, and by way of exception, the third. In an insignificant number of cases it happens that the fugue is an *andante* or *largo* (3rd trio of Opus III).

These movements, in which the bass enters into the imitative texture on the same footing and plan as the upper voices, have, as Professor Bukofzer observes (*op. cit.,* p. 232), great importance in the formation of the complex harmonic idiom which characterizes the chamber music of Corelli.

In plain truth, that which Corelli's contemporaries designated with the name of fugue in his work corresponds but rarely with what came to be understood by the term much later in the classical epoch. Sometimes it is a simple fugato with exact conformities, sometimes a canon at the unison or the fifth which is sustained for a few measures, then continues by more or less rigid imitations; sometimes a regular fugal entry is proposed with a formal subject and countersubject. Most of the time, save for a few fugues in Opus III, we encounter a fugato which is often worked in detail but is yet far from following a plan as strictly determined as that of the fugues of the *Wohltemperiertes Clavier.* "It is worth noting," says Professor Bukofzer, "that the fugal movements often sound more polyphonic than they actually are because of numerous redundant entries which merely pretend to introduce a new voice—a favorite Italian device that can be found as early as Frescobaldi." However, we are already far from the primitive canzone to which Sir Hubert Parry compared the *fugato* of Corelli in the article "Sonata" in the 1928 edition of Grove's *Dictionary.*

The movements which carry repeats—all the dances of the chamber trios and eight movements of the church trios patently derived from the courante, minuet, and gigue—are either of binary or ternary construction.

Movements of the binary type are composed in two sections of more or less equal dimensions separated by the repeat sign, and meant, therefore, to be repeated. Sometimes the two sections begin in the principal key (*allemanda* of Trio No. 3, Opus II); sometimes the first section ends on the dominant and the second section must then modulate to finish in the principal key (*sarabanda* of Trio No. 5, Opus II).

The ternary type subdivides into two categories. Its three sections may be arranged as in the aria with da capo, the third section strictly reproducing the first. In such cases the first section must of necessity terminate in the principal key. This type is not employed in the trios, but was used in the sonatas for violin and bass (the *tempo di gavotta* of Sonata No. 9, Opus V) in which pieces the middle section is written in the relative key.

Or else, as is most frequently the case, the first section ends in the relative key: it must inevitably branch off after its restatement, in order that the final cadence occur in the principal key (the *tempo di gavotta* Trio No. 8, Opus II).

Whether the construction be binary or ternary, the trio or sonata of Corelli never in any way foreshadows the discovery which a short time later endowed the sonata form with its significance and life: that of a second subject whose absolute contrast with the first opens up the field to developments of a hitherto unsuspected richness, to conflict of a dramatic intensity which Beethoven will carry to its highest point. Curiously enough, the Corellian fugue does actually contrast a subject and countersubject essentially different in rhythm and character: apart from this the counterpoint of slow movements, like that of the brisk dances, renounces this factor of variety. Rhythms and note-values engender either similar rhythms and note-values or ones that are so closely related that their possible combinations are rapidly exhausted. However, in the exploitation of these rather slender resources much ingenuity is used. For example, in the 9th trio of Opus

IV the *tempo di gavotta*, elsewhere limited to two repeated sections of four measures each (1st trio of Opus II), expands, becoming thereby an organized composition in which the middle phase is evolved by ideas adroitly derived from the theme. This is again the case with the *gigue* of the 4th trio of Opus IV. Here the first section contains, if not two subjects, at least a theme neatly divided into two parts, the first of which remains in the principal key and the second of which modulates to the dominant. In the second section we find, to begin with, rhythms germane to that of the principal theme but invested with new melodic contours; then an interplay of imitations which modulate to usher in the tonic; and then the gigue concludes with a restatement, not of the initial theme, but of some few bars with which the first section drew to a close, reappearing in the principal key.

Finally, there is a procedure which perhaps reveals a dim prescience of the law of contrasts to which the classical sonata will conform: it is that of interpolating *adagios* of a few measures' length in *allegro* movements, as in those of the 12th trio of Opus III. In this way a fantasia-like pattern is obtained with impromptu transition from vivacity to gravity, from agitation to contemplation, in a far less symmetrical manner than, for instance, in the *grave* of the 1st sonata of Opus V where the alternation of tempi brings to mind the usual equilibrium of the Venetian overture. But in the rare cases where these short *adagio* passages are regularly spaced throughout the *allegro*, there occurs a balancing, as it were, whose full periodicity becomes rhythmic.

Yet none of the constructions hitherto examined is the copyright of Corelli. The most elaborate of them are found in certain dances at the beginning of the seventeenth century. To cite only one example, the courante *Avogadrina* of Biagio Marini, 1620 (in *L'Arte musicale in Italia* by Torchi, VII, 3) is composed thus:

A section "A" of thirteen measures, twice stated, which opens in *g* and finishes in *B*-flat.

A section "B" of seven measures, which replies to "A," commencing in *B*-flat and closing in *g*.

A third and new section "C" of sixteen measures which retraces a contrary tonal trajectory.

Finally, a repeat of "B," which concludes the movement in the opening tonality.

As to the scale of composition, such a piece as the passacaglia of the *Artificii musicali* (1689) by Giovanni Battista Vitali is more than twice as extended as the longest inspiration of the four sets of trios, namely the ciacona concluding Opus II.[58] If one turns to the German school, the collections of Johann Jakob Walther published in 1676 and 1688 yield nothing to those of the master of Fusignano in matters of contrivance and inspiration.

Corelli's merit lies rather in the discrimination with which he employs the resources which are put at his disposal by the technique of his time, and in the choice of his materials. In the first place the themes are of great variety of outline, despite occasional clichés which are not palpably more tedious than the immutable final cadences with which the classics have had to make do for three centuries. Corelli's themes range from unconstrained melody amenable to clear-cut repeats to the abstraction of the fugal subject, less interesting for its own shape than for the suppleness which it shows in bending to the shapes to which the laws of its form condemn it.

There is no doubt that the contemporaries of Corelli, preferred the fugal type. Because of its departure from the plain formulas of song and popular dance, it appeared to them more worthy of the majesty of the sacred edifice; furthermore, it maintained the spirit of vocal polyphony which was traditional in the church, which instrumental music was only just beginning to oust in a discreet way, and not without resistance.

Corelli creates, with quite a special facility, themes for fugue and canon, which are so well adapted for their purpose that J. S. Bach was to use again, note for note, the subject and countersubject of a *vivace* from the 4th trio of Opus III in a Fugue in *b* (*Works for Organ*, Peters Edition, IV, 50).[59] Even in the chamber trios and in movements of dance origin, such as the allemande or the gigue, he manages to employ themes amenable to inversion, augmentation, and canonic exposition: the allemande of the 5th trio of Opus II is, at first, a canon in unison at a measure's interval; its second section states the theme in inversion, and this too is made to enter in canon at the unison.

Corelli also had a liking for descending chromatic themes (11th trio, Opus I), on which Bach himself constructed more than one masterpiece. True enough, this chromaticism had been in great favor with the forerunners of Corelli. The splendid *Sonata cromatica* for organ by Tarquinio Merula (printed by Torchi in *L'Arte Musicale in Italia*, III), *La Cornara* sonata by Legrenzi (1655), and a *Baletto* by Bassani (1677), among many other examples, show us chromaticism being exploited with an eloquent insistence.

It would be as well at this point to note more closely the part that such masters or rivals as Bassani, Torelli, Vitali, Maurizio Cazzati, Laurenti, Pietro degli Antoni—all those whom Vatielli groups into an early Bolognese School which was singularly rich and productive—may have played in the formation of Corelli's genius.

If on the title pages of his early works Corelli called himself "The Bolognese," this was not a mere phrase, but the asserted claim of an affiliation of whose full worth he was conscious.

It was to these but slightly known musicians (one is hardly engrossed by Laurenti or degli Antoni, and barely more so by Cazzati), and perhaps in a specific degree to Bassani, that Corelli owed the device of working out a theme otherwise than by repeating it at the dominant, although this sometimes occurs when he wants to stress the theme vigorously, as at the beginning of the 2nd trio, Opus I.

5.

For the most part Corelli's melody is characterized by a continuity, a replication, the secret of which the School of Bologna could have given him—in so far as a single group had anything to do with it. Such a theme as that of the *grave* in the Sonata in A major, No. 6, Opus V, is in the exact rhythm of the themes to be found in the sonatas *La Strozza* and *La Varana* of Opus XVIII of Cazzati (1656). An example of this form of writing is to be found on page 66, in which the theme, once it has been announced, is maintained by progressions, generally syncopated and of great nobility of contour. The defect of this is a certain monotony which is very difficult to avoid, since one has at one's disposal only a rather limited range of modulations. But besides the fact that this monotony must have been less obvious to more ingenuous listeners than those of the twentieth century, compensation was undoubtedly found in the beauty of the sonorities which this genre of writing affords as the voices literally interlace one with another, diverge, and conjoin in an interplay lasting to the final cadence. There is hardly any point in commenting on the plasticity of interpretation which this type of melody requires. Those who, on the strength of a stupid tradition, repeat that "Corelli and Vivaldi only knew one sort of conventional effect which consisted in the repetition of a phrase *piano* after it had been heard *forte*" [60] have never thought what incompatability exists between the puerile alternation of *forte* and *piano* and the *crescendo* and *diminuendo* implicit in such sequences.

Another influence less frequently affirmed, though at the same time as palpable, is that of the French; on the one hand Lully and the first composers of opera-ballet, and on the

other the more popular music of those violin bands to whom
all the courts of Europe had recourse. These latter are encountered in a certain number of sarabandes, allemandes,
courantes, and gavottes which are in the main short, with less
finely worked texture, but with straightforward and decisive
rhythms. By contrast it is Lully who appears in certain
largos written with energetic, heavily dotted rhythm, sound-
ing like opera overtures. Such largos are those of trios 2, 3,
and 11 of Opus II, and 3 and 4 Opus III. The prelude of
the 1st trio of Opus IV echoes for us even the favorite
modulation of Lully, his veritable signature:

6.

The German influence on the themes of Corelli is especially
apparent in the fugues of Opus V. It is, however, already

discernible in the *adagio* of the 1st trio of Opus IV: this design of repeated eighth-notes, which is to be found again in the concerti grossi, Opus VI, is that of a prelude by Johann Jakob Walther in the *Hortulus chelicus* of 1688. It was familiar to the masters beyond the Rhine, and J. S. Bach later recalls it in one of his sonatas for harpsichord and violin (Peters, No. 233, sonata V).

At times Corelli sought to consolidate the unity of his trios by maintaining an affinity between the themes of various movements. Such affinity exists in Opus I between the two *allegros* of the 10th trio, in Opus II between the *largo, allemanda,* and *corrente* of the 1st trio; between the *largo,* the *allegro,* and *presto* of the 3rd; between the *adagio,* the *allemanda,* and *tempo di gavotta* of the 8th; and in Opus V between the celebrated *gavotta* in *F* of the 10th sonata and the *giga* which follows it.

This anticipation of the cyclic principle on which two centuries hence an entire school of composition would be based was anything but novel even at the time of Corelli. The pavane and galliard in twin arrangement for the lutenists and harpsichordists of the sixteenth century afford us many examples of it. In the seventeenth century one often finds the corrente which follows a balletto utilizing the latter's theme with a slackened rhythm, in quite another manner from a simple variation. The German, Peurl, in his book of *Pavanes, Intrade, Danses et gaillardes* composed about 1611 and published in 1620, wrote entire suites with the same melodic material presented with four different rhythmical aspects. Among the Italian violinists Biagio Marini excelled at this artifice (see *Il Priulino* of 1620, in Torchi, VII) as Bassani and Vitali were to do later on. Harpsichord players and organists yielded them nothing in this practice: this may be judged from the following short extract from Frescobaldi, taken from his *Toccate d'Intavolatura di cimbalo et organo* (Book I, Rome, 1637):

7.

Balletto

Corrente del Balletto

To complete this brief review of the thematic material of Corelli, it would be necessary to speak here of the ornamentation with which it was the custom to grace the slow movements and sometimes even the *allegros*. We shall do this more pertinently in respect to Opus V, for which we have abundant evidence.

If we now consider the movement of voices in relation to one another, we find ourselves in the presence of one of the most significant aspects of Corelli's genius. With the publication of his trios his mastery of composition had been acknowledged; the criticisms of Lecerf de la Viéville, about which we shall have a word to say later, remained isolated instances without any general echo, and it must be admitted that they are paltry in the extreme.

Francesco Gasparini, a theorist of repute, was not merely discharging the indebtedness of pupil to master when he praised Corelli, "true Orpheus of our time" (as early as 1689 Bernardi had called him "the new Orpheus of our time"), for being the most adept musician at "introducing and modulating his basses with so much art, study, and charm," for preparing and ingeniously resolving dissonances, and for interlacing his subjects, which are so varied that in him there is to be truly discerned "the inventor of a perfect, bewitching harmony." [61] Very much later Arteaga declared him the greatest harmonist who had ever lived in Italy, and listed as characteristics of his school "contrivance and mastery in imitations, suppleness of modulations, contrast between the various voices, simplicity and charm of harmony." As for Avison, the best "modern" composers were indebted to Corelli for the elements of their harmony.

Concerning the actual term "harmony," the knowledge already acquired of Corelli's style, in so far as the trios are concerned, precludes there being any misapprehension. The reigning spirit in these works is counterpoint. The figuring of the basses indicates a clear perception of the "harmonic situation," so to speak, at each instant of development. But while in Opera V and VI, which are resolutely modern in spirit, it happens that chordal progressions are subordinated to the melodic line, investing it with color and a new ambiance, the harmonies of the trios result from the motion of the voices: they are neither enhanced by any latitude nor could they be conceived as other than they are, at least in the slow movements and the more elaborated *allegros*.

This is hardly so where there is encountered, as in some *adagios* (Opus I, trios 3, 9, and 10), counterpoint in the first species, note against note, which gives the ear the impression of chordal harmonies struck and sustained. Movements thus begun develop generally in that style of syncopated imitations for which Corelli showed a constant predilection. In this respect how much more modern is the *largo* of Bassani printed by Vatielli, p. 170, in which the upper voice seems so free, the harmony so plastic, though the whole devolves on a *basso ostinato*.

However, we approach harmony in the modern sense in some of the dances of the chamber trios, the sarabandes, courantes, gavottes, if "modern" is understood in the significance given it by musicians of the eighteenth century who in opera and instrumental music declared war on the polyphony of the motet writers of former times. Curiously enough, some of the brisk dances, like the gigue, or those with a marked rhythm, like the allemande, are, on more than one occasion, still treated in the contrapuntal style. Also, the two methods are often combined, as if Corelli were contriving wittingly a progressive advance towards the emancipation which Opus V achieves in this respect.

At whatever stage of its evolution it is considered, the harmony of Corelli is simple, pellucid, and absolutely correct. Only the succession of fifths (Opus II, trio No. 3) which led to the arguments previously related between him and Colonna appears difficult to understand. F. T. Arnold rightly observed that a theorist like Marpurg, liberal as he might be, could not admit Corelli's explanation.[62] As to false relations, such as that with which the *adagio* of the 11th trio, Opus III, opens, the old usage was less strict, and the practices of ornamentation could assuage its effect in the simplest possible way.

8.

Finally, certain effects like that which F. T. Arnold [63] christened "a Corelli clash" almost result in impressionism. When in place of the usual cadence

9.

Corelli writes:

10.

it is not an inadvertence on his part, as the formula is used many times (Opus I, *adagio* of the 6th trio; Opus II, *allemanda* of the 2nd trio, *allemanda* and *tempo di gavotta* of the 5th, *allemanda* of the 6th, *preludio* and *sarabanda* of the 8th, and *largo* of the 9th; Opus IV, *sarabanda* of the 3rd trio, etc.). He seeks to give to this hackneyed phrase a new mordent, somewhat analogous to the piquancy of certain acciaccature.

In so doing he gives his preoccupations with sonority precedence over his scruples about form. Indeed, it seems obvious that he was more concerned with sonority than any of his predecessors. He has a liking for a certain full, homogenous quality in which rare accentuations of the type of this unexpected "clash" intervene to enhance a polish and equilibrium without parallel. In the sonatas for solo violin he has recourse to virtuosity; the trios are adapted to a less exacting technique in order that the players can give each note full articulation.

The two upper parts are always in proximity, but on the other hand are separated from the bass by a wide interval: the realization of the continuo fills this space with harmony but leaves the gap between the interlinked sonorities of the two violins and that of the violoncello. The two soprano voices very often cross, as in most instrumental compositions of the time. In movements of homophonic tendency they frequently move at an interval of a third (Opus I, 2nd trio, opening of the *adagio;* Opus II, 1st trio, opening of the *preludio* and the *corrente;* 3rd trio, opening of the *preludio* and the *allemanda*). Among the most striking examples may be cited the *allegro* in 12/8 meter of the 10th trio, Opus III, entirely based on a parallelism of thirds in which the upper melodic line alternates ceaselessly between the first and second violin.

The tessitura within which the two violins range is strangely limited. For practical purposes it extends from the low *D* (third open string) to the fifteenth above, the first *D* on the E-string—say two octaves, half the actual compass of the instrument. The anti-virtuosity is unabashed; several trios could be performed in the first position, and the third position is never exceeded.

This proscription of the higher register is understandable from Corelli's love for full sonorities and facilitated technique. The reserve with which the lower register is treated is somewhat stranger. In Opus I alone, the 1st, 5th, and 7th trios do not have recourse to the G-string even for a single note. In the other trios a violin may plunge almost furtively as far as *C* or *B*, but very quickly returns to the middle register. It is true that this abstention is more or less a general thing. Some recondite German composers, among them Böddecker in 1651, though not daring to entrust any really sustained melodies to the G-string at least use it extensively as the base for their chords. The Italians, even the most daring of them, scarcely hazarded this much. Perhaps this was due partly to the way in which they held their violins, without chin rest or pad. And also undoubtedly because the period did not take kindly to the sonorities of the *bourdon*. The French were still using notes too deep for the liking of the Abbé Raguenet in 1702: "With us the upper voice is generally of sufficient beauty; but the lower voice could not be expected to have any, descending as low as it is made to do: in Italy the upper voices are written three or four tones higher than in France so that the second voices are thereby in a sufficiently high register to have as much beauty as our first voices themselves."

Very much later, a complete theory was advanced by Martinelli to explain Corelli's usage in his *Lettres familières;* I have previously given an inaccurate version of it on the testimony of an erring historian. Here is the restored passage almost in its entirety: [64]

If we come to inquire from whence comes this magical power of the compositions of Corelli, we shall very quickly find that their whole secret inheres in their marvellously imitating the most dulcet and pleasing characteristics of the human voice, and their contriving to express in sound the passions which a concert of human voices would express, each according to its range, and with regard to the most exact rules of art. The degrees of power of the human voice are as manifold as the diverse ages of man.

A dissertation on the evolution of the human voice follows, and then:

Pieces of instrumental music can only imitate a discourse indicative of some passion. The judicious performer will always be preoccupied with choosing sonorities most fitted to please the ears of his auditors. The shrill, strident, displeasing sounds of

infant voices are to be avoided above all: in their wailing the
newborn can only depict the expression of suffering to which
at their tender age they are incessantly exposed. Instrumental
players, and especially violinists, if they take account of this,
will carefully eschew these overshrill sounds, which they use
constantly in their ungrateful and profitless essays at bravura.
For joyous events youth is the appointed time, that is to say the
tempered soprano and the contralto: for the expression of love
the tenor is indeed suitable, but with more moderation. A serious
conversation is normally the act of more mature persons, and
can be expressed befittingly by the tenor, baritone, and bass.
In a concertante piece, where it may be imagined that all the
voices take part in the same conversation, the most strident,
which typify youth, should intervene less frequently, like those
persons who are dissuaded from much talk by their modesty.
This plan seems to have guided Corelli in all his compositions:
he entrusted the greater part of the interest to the middle voices
and then used the basses as regulators of the symphony; or, if
you will, the musical discourse. Although the most erudite masters in this art urged their pupils to take Corelli as their model
in imitating Nature, the latter, once they had achieved composer's status, did no less than abandon the golden road of these
middle registers, and not only began to use the most piercing,
puerile, and strident tones of their instrument, but, forsaking the
evocation of the human voice, started to imitate dogs, birds, or
other animals—and this they called bravura.

The explanation of Martinelli, overlaid by his whimsical
imageries, is not as absurd as it may seem. It offers a confused
insight into a characteristic of Corellian inspiration, later on
analyzed much better: this voluntary moderation, this desire
to offer nothing to the listener but what has been perfectly
worked out. With that one touches on an order of decorative
formal beauty, very well defined by Torrefranca when, in
respect to the sonatas and trios, he lays emphasis on the almost

visual quality of this music whose unfolding evokes "the sight of a frieze skirting the walls or pediment of a temple." [65] This is indeed the truth; and the parallelism of the trios' upper parts, broken by the interlacing which they trace in crossing, certainly has the value of a plastic motif.

Maroncelli, too zealous a biographer by far, proclaimed that before Corelli instrumental composition was in total barbarism, that no one knew how to give a bass part any design of musical interest, or how to make any parts other than the upper ones sing. If the exaggeration is a flagrant one, the fact remains that before Corelli the ensemble of voices had never been fashioned with such harmonious coherence.

THE SONATAS FOR VIOLIN AND BASS, OPUS V

Before the publication of Opus V at the beginning of 1700 —the dedication is dated the first of January—Corelli had undoubtedly written sonatas for solo violin and figured bass. The letter which he addressed to Count Laderchi on June 3, 1679, was for the purpose of announcing the dispatch of an unpublished sonata for violin and lute or violone.[66] But Opus V was actually the first and only collection which he published in this genre. He attached extreme importance to it, as though he had prescience of the preference which posterity would bestow on this work—not without injustice toward the others, particularly to the concerti grossi. Dr. Burney does not always warrant our complete confidence, but he can be believed when he writes: "I was told by Mr. Wiseman at Rome, that when he first arrived in that city, about twenty years after Corelli's decease he was informed by several persons who had been acquainted with him that his *Opera Quinta*, on which all good schools for the violin have since been founded, cost him three years to revise and correct" (III, 556).

Like the trios in the aggregate, Opus V is divided equally between church sonatas and the chamber sonatas. These are very clearly distinguished in the original edition in which the second part is separated from the first by a new title page with the following wording: *Parte seconda, Preludii, Alle-mande, Correnti, Gighe, Sarabande, Gavotte e Follia.*

Before endeavoring to define the essential features of these twelve sonatas, we will analyze briefly one of each type: the first one of the set, which is a church sonata, and the tenth in *F*, the fourth and most celebrated of the chamber sonatas which comprise the second part.

CHURCH AND CHAMBER SONATAS

1st Sonata in *D: Grave—Allegro—Allegro—Adagio— Allegro*

The first movement, a slow one segmented by two fast episodes, is very solidly constructed beneath its appearance of spontaneity. It opens with a slow phrase A, two measures in length, in the principal key: this phrase is brusquely cut short, as is often done in the Venetian operatic overture in the seventeenth century, by a sort of caprice of seven measures in rapid tempo which closes by cadencing in the dominant. Then, in a passage marked *adagio* a second slow motif B, a sequel to A, makes its appearance and also concludes with a dominant. The second section is symmetrical: the two measures of A are repeated in the dominant key, followed by the same caprice of seven measures transposed from *D* into *A* to terminate in *E*. The motif B then resumes in *E* and returns through *A* to the principal key of *D* in which the movement ends.

The first *allegro,* a fugato in common time, is also in *D*. After presentation of the theme, a short angular one in three parts (the first two entrusted to the violin, in double stopping), the play of imitations is carried on for about half the movement: the second half is devoted to violinistic virtuosity. This, from then on, consists only of arpeggios and variant broken chords, contrapuntal imitation playing no further part.

A second *allegro,* C meter, in *D* follows. It is a sort of *moto perpetuo* in sixteenth-notes of rather slight musical interest, although the logic of the modulations helps a melodic line evolve that is not quite vapid. Though it is the custom of those rare virtuosi who play this *allegro* in public to interpret it with that frigid portentiousness which unmistakably suggests the respectability of Corelli, one is tempted to see in the variety of figuration an invitation to variety of bowing: full *détaché* bowing at the opening; *martelé* in the 5th and 6th measures, for example; *sautillé* in the 8th and 9th measures before the end. But to do this it is imperative to renounce a pseudoclassical tradition which did not die with Spohr. In the presence of the word "*spiccato*" in a sonata by Corelli, a commentator declared at a relatively recent date: "I would not dream of allowing the pupil to raise his bow from the string, or to jump it, or to do any other of those French bowing tricks which were first thought of something more than a century after Corelli's death." *

* James Brown in *The Music Teacher,* London, December, 1925.

Adagio, 3/2, in *b.* A slow movement in Corelli's most beautiful vein. Let us reserve for separate consideration the question of ornaments which might be superimposed on the original melody. Here the air has a broad enough sweep to be self-sufficient. It is a lyrical effusion, even elegiac, without any other symmetrical feature than its rhythm—the phrase surges forward by progressions and modulations in which academic writing has no part. The *adagio* ends on the chord of the dominant of *B* which links up, as so often happens in Bach and Handel, with the *D* of the finale.

Allegro, 6/8, in *D.* This in inspiration is analogous to the first *allegro,* whose theme is taken up again, apart from the rhythm, and restated by imitation in the same way. An episode of sheer virtuosity in rapid figuration succeeds the double stopping. A recurrence of fugal writing brings the work to a close.

10TH SONATA IN *F: Preludio—Allemanda—Sarabanda— Gavotta—Giga*

Preludio, C, in *F* (*adagio*). The theme is a thinly disguised variant of the *grave* of the 6th sonata: its development utilizes little more than the elements of Corelli's idiomatic vocabulary.

Allemanda, C, in *F* (*allegro*). Analogous to that of the 8th sonata. It is a very close relation of the prelude: the two themes have the same skeletal structure, the same rhythm, and in the course of the allemande there often appears a dactyl rhythm borrowed from the prelude.

Sarabanda, 3/4, in *F* (*largo*). In two sections of the normal Corellian type. The rhythm is quite foreign to that which generally characterizes the sarabande. No long note-values, but a design of quarter-notes and eighth-notes which, were it to be detached from the bass, would suit a *Ländler*. By means of widely-spaced broken chords the violin plays its own accompaniment without double stopping at the tenth below.

Gavotta, C, in *F* (*allegro*). This is the famous gavotte later extended by variation by Tartini under the title *L'Arte dell'Arco*. Very short—two sections of four measures separated by the repeat sign—its merit lies in its irresistible sincerity which very soon made it popular (*see* page 39).

Giga, 6/8, in *F* (*allegro*). In two asymmetrical sections; the second is none other than the theme of the *gavotta* rhythmically changed and stated in its entirety, with a brusque modulation in the theme's last measure to *d*, initiating a development to which the *gavotta,* limited by its own directness, could not lend itself.

La Follia

Just as Opus II ended with a chaconne and variations, Opus V puts in the place of a sixth and last chamber sonata 23 variations on the *follia*. The importance which violinists, rightly or wrongly, attribute to this *follia*, the errors of interpretation to which it has given rise, would detain us rather longer than its intrinsic musical interest would warrant. Its interest being, in our opinion, purely pedagogical, we will examine it a little later on at the same time as the other technical contributions of Opus V.

While the trios of Opera I to IV referred back particularly to the earlier polyphonic type, tempered though they were and carried to a high degree of perfection by Corelli, Opus V is oriented, still somewhat cautiously, toward the homophonic style and toward virtuosity.[67] It will furnish us with important information on the technique of the violin in such light as its composer conceived this subject. As for form, Opus V is not appreciably different from that of the trios. As may be figured out from the earlier brief analysis, the apportionment and grouping of the church sonatas and the chamber sonatas is the same for Opus V as for Opera I to IV. Terminology remains the same save for the disappearance of the *andante* and *presto*, as the following table makes evident:

Movements	Church Sonatas (1 to 6)	Chamber Sonatas (7 to 12)
Grave	3	
Adagio	9	2
Allegro	13	1
Vivace	5	1
Preludio		5
Allemanda		2
Corrente		1
Sarabanda		3
Gavotta		3
Giga	1	4
Follia		1

It will be observed that the two *adagios* of the chamber sonatas (sonatas 9 and 11) are mere bridge passages of eight and nine measures respectively; the *vivace* (sonata 11) is rhythmically a gigue, but contrapuntally designed; and the *allegro* (sonata 11), as was stated earlier, is a gavotte with freely treated variations. On the other hand, the church sonatas allow the intrusion of gigues—finale *allegro* of the 3rd sonata, and the *giga*, expressly designated as such, of the 5th. Note the abnormal position of the *giga* of the 9th sonata, where it appears as a second movement instead of being placed at the end in the normal way.

The respective disposition of the various movements is virtually the same as in Opera I to IV. The church sonatas of Opus V all comprise five movements, while of the chamber sonatas, three are in four movements, and two are in five; for the sixth sonata is substituted variations on the *follia*. If we again take the designation *S* for slow movements and *F* for fast, we find in the church sonatas four works of the type *S F S S F* and two of the type *S F S F F*. This latter schema is also that of two chamber sonatas (10 and 11); two other sonatas belong to the type *S F S F*, and one to type *F F S F*. The succession of two fast movements is not so illogical as may seem at first sight. In the chamber sonatas the highly differentiated rhythms of the dances afford an appreciable element of contrast. In the church sonatas with two consecutive *allegros*, the first is always fugal and of relatively severe character; the second is homophonic, brisk, finely spun, and could be regarded as a scherzo before its time.

The tonal unity remains as strong as in the trios. Out of eleven sonatas (excluding the *follia*), three have all their movements in the same key, and the remaining eight only make an exception for the central adagio, written in the relative key.

Perhaps at this stage it would not be unprofitable to emphasize the role of Corelli in the "installation" of the major-minor tonality which has dominated all music of the eighteenth and nineteenth centuries, and which has still not exhausted its potentialities in the span of nearly a half century during which atonality has waged a campaign against it.

According to Professor Bukofzer (*op. cit.*, p. 222) "Arcangelo Corelli . . . can take the credit for the full realization of tonality in the field of instrumental music. His works

auspiciously inaugurate the period of late baroque music."
This assertion may surprise us; modern tonality has some very
remote precursors. From the Middle Ages onward (Pérotin,
Pierre de la Croix, Moniot d'Arras, in the 13th century) certain pieces were subordinated to the principle in a sporadic
way, or even perhaps by chance. In the seventeenth century,
among the first Italian composers of sonatas the feeling for
modality had well-nigh atrophied to the gain of the major-
minor concept, which in nowise was ambiguous in the works
of Biagio Marini, Cazzati, and others.

Corelli's originality and efficacy of action derived from his
being the first to use sequential formulas while ceding to them
in full measure their obviousness, as in the case of the descending series of first inversions which present the degrees
of the diatonic scale in systematic order, thereby clearly de-
fining tonality:

11.

Op. V, 7th sonata, measures 59–66 of the Corrente

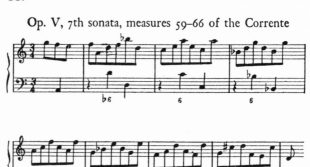

Professor Bukofzer, from whom I have borrowed these
observations (p. 220), adds that the possibility of interrupting

these sequences at any point offers at the same time a simple means of modulating. Seen in this light, tonality, having been affirmed by patterns of this order or by those determined by the "circle of fifths," established a graduated system of chordal relations between a tonal center (the tonic triad in major or minor) and the other triads (or seventh chords) of the diatonic scale. None of these chords was in itself new, but they now served a new function, namely that of circumscribing the key.

In the construction of the various sonata movements more variety is found than the trios reveal; also more maturity. The *gavotta* of the 9th sonata gives us in its purity the schema A-B-A with full *da capo* of the A theme. If the first and second subject concept is not yet in sight, at least we are already in the presence—in the *allegro* of the 11th sonata—of a definite "first movement" with its theme ending in a cadence in the dominant key, a short modulatory development, and thematic recapitulation in the tonic key.

Nonetheless, Corelli does not greatly diverge on the whole from the prototypes that were offered him by his immediate predecessors, Venetian and Lombard. When he interposed rapid episodes in the *grave* of the 1st sonata, which evoke for Heuss the influence of the Venetian operatic sinfonia,[68] perhaps Corelli was reminded of similar sallies in the *adagios* of the Bolognese Laurenti whose Opus I had appeared in 1691. In his thematic material the Bolognese influences are still more apparent, in particular those of Pietro degli Antoni, Laurenti, and Maurizio Cazzati; this last was a native of Guastalla who had been educated at Ferrara and Bergamo but who wrote the best part of his instrumental music at Bologna. Vatielli has studied these sources with great discernment. As for Bassani, his affinities with Corelli in his themes as well as in the molding and development of phrase have already attracted the attention of Dr. Burney. Corelli's virtue is that he blended the diverse tendencies into a homogenous unity, animated not by the fervor and fantasy Fausto Torrefranca would admire in the work, but by a vitality intense enough to rise above the deadweight of formulas, made beautiful by a wonderful balance of inspiration and technical ability.

TECHNIQUE

We have no reliable contemporary witness to the technique of Corelli. All those eulogies in which he is Apollo, Orpheus, or Christopher Columbus remain equally vague. We only know that his virtuosity, however modest it may seem to us, was esteemed very highly. An account of a fête given by the *Accademia dei Arcadi* extols him as a leader of the orchestra, and then tells us that he was more marvelous still when he began to play solo.[69] According to Hawkins (II, 674), to whom we owe the curious details about Corelli's mode of life mentioned earlier, "the style of his playing was learned, elegant, and pathetic, and his tone firm and even: Mr. Geminiani, who was well acquainted with and had studied it, was used to resemble it to a sweet trumpet."

In Opus V, the faithful résumé of his researches and the pellucid expression of his ideal, we shall find the most trustworthy account of Corelli's playing.

Bowing: La follia

The bowing technique of Corelli is revealed in all its aspects in the *follia*, apart from certain *bariolages*, an example of which is to be found in the 3rd sonata, and some arpeggio passages in the first two. (See example 19, page 108.)

At the outset we will recount briefly the historical background of the *follia*, for a misappreciation of it is likely to affect in an odd way the musical significance attributed to the work. In fact, the majority of modern transcribers have let themselves be overawed by the title with its truly dangerous suggestions. Thomson does not conceal that he has "spent years in assessing the profundity of this work," [70] in which he discerns a description of madness; like Tartini composing his "Devil's Trill" sonata, Corelli was supposed to have painted in sound the most awful of mental crises.

Now the theme of the *follia* (or *folia*, for both spellings occur) does not belong to Corelli; the idea of madness is irrelevant to it, and the calmest of composers certainly has done nothing to integrate such a concept in the work. The *follias* are thought to have been known in Portugal as early as the fourteenth century from the time of Don Pedro the First, who, it was said, danced them "with passion." They probably originated in that country.

The eminent Portuguese musicologist Luis de Freitas-Branco, whom I have consulted in the matter, stresses the point that because of the Portuguese origins of the *follias*, the substantive *folia* (obsession), as well as the verb *foliar*, which derives from it, are both part of the Portuguese vernacular, although Spanish does not possess them.

Though from the beginning of the seventeenth century it was customary to assign a Spanish origin to the *follias* (their title from then on was almost invariably *folies d'Espagne*), a number of lexicographers and classical Spanish writers de-

fine the *follia* as "a Portuguese dance." And the first definition
of them given by a theorist—a Spaniard, Francesco Salinas,
in his treatise *De Musica*—is drafted thus: "Ut ostenditur in
vulgaribus quas Lusitani *Follias* vocant, ad hoc metri genus
[the Sapphic meter] et ad hunc canendi modum institutis,
qualis est illa, cujus cantus usitatus est": [71]

12.

Lusitani, in a Spanish text of 1577, clearly indicates the
Portuguese, and one cannot see how Joaquin Nin (*Musico-
grafia*, 1935, Monovar) has been able to deduce from them a
case in favor of Spanish origin.

As a matter of fact, these questions of priority lose much
of their importance in the light of the remarks of Otto
Gombosi [72] on the undeniable affinities which exist between
the ostinato pattern of the *follias* and those of the *passamezzo
antico* and the *romanesca* whose earliest notations predate
those of the oldest *follias*.

It was not the theme quoted above in Example 12 which
was destined much later to become characteristic of the
follias. It existed already in a latent state in some binary
dances, such as these *pavanes* of Alphonso Mudurra which
date from 1546:

...cangelo Corelli; engraving by John Smith from the painting by H. Howard.

Cardinal Pietro Ottoboni, the p
of Corelli, Alessandro Scarlatti, and
nardo Pasquini.

Francesco Geminiani (1687–
1762), Corelli's greatest pupil.
Later as a virtuoso and composer
he was Corelli's indefatigable prop-
agandist.

13.

It was also lightly sketched out in a pavane in triple meter by Enriquez de Valderrábano, *Silva de Sirenas* (1547):

14.

The identification of the title with this time-honored theme took place at the end of the sixteenth century. At this point the *follias* were introduced into a number of collections of instrumental music where they were always treated as variations on an ostinato bass. It is not known for certain what the character of the theme was originally: according to Paul Nettl [73] it was quick, but in the seventeenth century it was assuredly reduced to a very moderate tempo. The *follia* was then a stately dance, performed by a solo dancer, and related to the slow sarabande and to the chaconne. *Follias* are to be found in the *Partite* of Frescobaldi (1614), in the *Scherzi amorsi* of Giovanni Stefani (1622), in the *Secondo Scherzo delle Ariose vaghe* of Carlo Milanuzzi (1625), the *Dodici Chitarre spostate* of Francesco Sabatini (1643), in the *Galeria musicale . . . compartita in diversi Scherzi di Chitarriglia* of Stefano Pesori of Mantua (1648), in the *Quattro libri della Chitarra spagnuola* of the Academician Caliginoso, called the Raging (before 1650), in *Il Primo Libro di Canzone* of Andrea Falconieri (1650), the *Selva di varie Composizioni d'Intavolatura per cimbalo ed organo* of Bernard Storace (1664), in the *Arie per il balletto a cavallo* of Schmelzer (1667) in the *Instrucción de Musica* of Gaspar Sanz (1674), in a manuscript of the lutanist Béthune (about 1680, library of the Paris Conservatoire), in the *Pièces de luth composées . . . par Jacques de Gallot avec les Folies d'Espagne enrichies de plusiers beaux couplets* (Ecorcheville collection, 1670–1680), and in the *Division Violin* of Playford (1684) under the title of *Faronell's Division on a Ground*.

By that time *follias* had become so commonplace that Robert de Visée refrained from introducing them into his

Livre de guittare [*sic*] of 1682: "One will certainly not come across any more *Folies d'Espagne*," he wrote. "So many strains of them abound, cluttering up all the concerts, that I should only be repeating the follies of others." But d'Anglebert was not disconcerted by this craze, and produced twenty-two "Variations sur les Folies d'Espagne" in his *Pièces de clavecin* of 1689; variations were likewise written by Pasquini, and later by Marin Marais, Vivaldi, Guignon, and C. Ph. E. Bach. As for Spain, the *Catalogue of Music in the Biblioteca Nacional at Madrid*, by Higinio Angles and José Subira, Volume I, "Manuscripts" (Barcelona, 1946) mentions eight *folies* with variations for organ, harpsichord, harp, and guitar, composed between 1705 and 1721, among them being some *Folias graves* and some *Folias Ytalianas*.

Although stylized and learnedly treated by the masters, the *follias* were not neglected by choreographers. Mme. de Sévigné in a letter of the 24th of July, 1689, to Mme. de Grignan, described a ball at which there danced "the son of this Senechal of Rennes [Charles du Lys] who was so wild, and had had so many adventures. . . . He danced those beautiful chaconnes, the *Folies d'Espagne*, but particularly the passepied, with his wife with a perfection, with an accomplishment, which is indescribable."

The vogue of the theme of the *follia* persisted for a long time in Brittany, for a Member of the Convention, Honoré Fleury, born at Quintin in 1754, recalled having danced them at the age of nine on the occasion of an entertainment given by the masters of his college (Saint-Brieuc).[74] They were no less popular in Germany, where Farinelli (for a long time settled in Hanover) probably brought them into fashion. In a Hamburg opera of 1690, *Die grossmüthige Thalestris*, a wag exclaims: ". . . that which now must befit men of gallantry, to wit the follies of Spain." Whereon a servant brings him a guitar, and he plays the air in question.[75] Tablatures like those of C. Grimm, in 1698, also included some *folies d'Espagne*.

Information on several other versions of the *follia* will be found in the notes; what has just been stated suffices to show clearly that the Corellian setting was in no respect revolutionary in character. For the composer it was a case of rounding off a collective work, impatiently awaited, in a superlative manner with a composition of academic perfection, capable of arousing astonishment not by its novelty or dramatic intensity but by its unusual breadth of proportion and by the wealth of knowledge implied in its writing.

The form of air with variations was the only one which allowed Corelli to dilate to such degree that his action became virtually the art of construction. An effort to minimize inevitable monotony is discernible in the set of 23 variations, particularly by giving to the accompaniment as active a role as possible. Several times in the 3rd variation and in the 16th the same designs are exchanged between melody and bass. Sometimes this reciprocity operates between groups of two variations; for example, between the 4th and 5th, 6th and 7th, 20th and 21st. Still more revealing is the manner in which the ostinato of the bass is now and then halted. The harmonic framework of the 14th variation is new, likewise that of the 19th, which is in imitation with supple modulations, and that of the 20th, which cadences in *F* while the 21st variation traverses the reversed key sequence. Finally, an elongation

by four measures at the close of the last phase attests, by itself, to Corelli's desire to evade customary routine and to invest a somewhat naive architecture with a degree of nobility.

But there is no doubt, as is evident from a cursory reading
of the *follia*, that in Corelli's eyes its interest was of a violinistic
order before all else. Everything he knew about the matter
of instrumental technique, which he had scattered throughout Opus V, and the device of variation, enabled him to concentrate, to classify, and to demonstrate with precision in a
veritable corpus of doctrine. By technique, that of bowing
should be understood; for as regards the left hand, Corelli's
role, as we shall shortly see, far from being constructive, was
limited to "pruning."

The first three variations deal with bowing strokes of de-
creasing length—*détaché* full-bow, *détaché* half-bow, and
then with third- or quarter-bow. The end of the 3rd variation
combines the difficulty of the triplet with that of the asym-
metric tied note; the 4th variation has reference to broken
chord figuration with addition of double stopping in the
upper part; this study also provides roughly the material for
numbers 5, 7, and 23; the 6th variation, a design of arpeggios,
requires the *sautillé* stroke. The 8th variation is devoted to
eighth-notes slurred in twos; the 9th to short and incisive
détaché bowing; the 10th to crossing the strings; the 11th to
prolonged notes, both sustained as double stopping. The 12th
variation may require the *martelé* stroke; the indication is not
expressly given by Corelli, but in all the teaching derived
from his *modus operandi* a comparable design is traditionally
performed with this bowing in mind. The other variations

have similar problems as their aim. One deserves particular attention—the 14th variation, appearing thus in the original edition:

15.

Nowadays, arrangers follow Ferdinand David and substitute for these few notes an impassioned air on the G-string:

16.

The role of this effusion in the dramatic thread of the *follia* is perceived without undue difficulty; the demented wretch, after a series of eccentricities—duly related by the arranger, who seasons the restrained variations of Corelli with pizzicati and arpeggios attacked from a grace note as manifestations of cerebral derangement—the demented wretch, then, having momentarily recovered his sanity, moans over the sadness of his destiny: the *lamento espressivo* on the G-string is there for no other purpose.

But we have seen apropos the trios that neither Corelli nor his contemporaries—nor, we could add, his successors for at least two generations—ever gave a sustained air to the G-string. And if ever the occasion were fitting for not ornamenting an *adagio*, it was when a master of technique in the midst of a series of bowing problems tackled that one which was considered in those days the most ticklish of all: the playing of a sustained note. Wishing to give Somis the finest eulogy he could, Hubert Le Blanc wrote in 1740: "He cleared the post where people come to grief, in short he succeeded in the great feat on the violin of *holding a whole-note*." [76]

These dotted half-notes tied in pairs were in their place in the middle of a *follia*, a work completely analogous in concept to Tartini's gavotte with variations. Each of these two works exactly renders an account of an era of the *Art of Bowing*, determining its tendencies and limits.

For this reason the success which greeted the *follia* is understandable. Vivaldi wrote one at the end of his first work (circa 1707); another Venetian, Giovanni Reali, dedicated his *Sonate e capricci . . . con una Follia* (1709) to Corelli, whom he acclaimed in his preface, saluting him as the Christopher Columbus of music; Nicolo Sanguinazzo composed, under the transparent pseudonym of Olocin Ozzaniugnas, Diletante (*sic*) di Violoncello, a *Partita di Folie, tutte sopra un Basso* wherein the theme is varied thirty-one times, just as many variations as in the remarkable *Couplets de Folies* of Marin Marais (second book of *Pièces de Viole*, 1701).

It is more difficult to explain the permanence of the success of the *follia* and the welcome which continues to be extended in public performance to its transcriptions, all more or less derivative from Ferdinand David's, which is based on a mis-conception; and to new compositions inspired by a work which, in Riehl's opinion, is "the most feeble and sorry" that Corelli produced. Liszt, Sivori,[77] and later Manuel Ponce and Rachmaninoff (1931) paid their homage to it. Perhaps it is on account of the sombre beauty of the theme and of the prestige attached to the name of its so-called composer. Yet in this instance this prestige is usurped: the true composer of these sixteen measures will never be known. Corelli's merit is that he utilized them, perhaps less ingeniously than Marais, but with a didactic rigor thanks to which his *follia* constitutes a model study, an exact antithesis of that inspired rhapsody which David and Thomson were pleased to see in it.

Left Hand Technique

A complete idea of the bowing technique of Corelli can be construed from the *follia*. It is essentially an "evolving" (*ouverte*) technique in the sense that its few and simple enough elements, which were culled from the Bolognese and other predecessors of Arcangelo, yet definitely co-ordinated by him, are amenable to development and infinite ramification. In the process of development of bow technique, objectives are laid down by its rational partitioning: broken chords, crossing of the strings, arpeggios, tied notes, all presuppose a flexibility sufficiently evolved so that the very much more complex passages of Tartini, or even of Locatelli, may be de-rived from them in a natural way. There is also no question of the absurd restraint of the down-bow at the start of each measure in the contemporary French style, or of any other stereotyped practice whatsoever; the emancipation acquired at the cost of assiduity, for which the *follia* gives us the method, puts the interpreter in a position to translate the smallest nuances of the musical discourse, and to subordinate entirely his performance to the intentions of the composer.

This very sentiment of deference toward the music has consequences almost opposed to those which stem from the technique of the left hand. With that approach the nascent violin schools had naturally succumbed to the same tendency always apparent in virtuosi in their novitiate: with the bowing mastered little or not at all, without variety or lissomeness to let oneself be carried away by rapid passages or by the scaling of the upper register. Now, as Fausto Torrefranca has said, instrumental art in Italy, seeking to refine the old counterpoint for enhancement of the melody, "in lyrically emancipating the upper voice, that of the violin, could not go beyond a certain point without falling into the void of virtuosity." Some of Corelli's forerunners, the German Walther, and the Bohemian Biber, whose entire technique astounds us by its maturity and boldness, knew, in the degree that they surmounted the difficulty, how to avoid this risk. For the majority of violinists the menace was not illusory. Corelli saw it clearly, and from the outset maintained a reactionary attitude.

As far back as 1649, Marco Uccellini in Italy had tackled the 6th position: [78]

17.

The *Musurgia* of Kircher, published the following year, fixed the upper limit of the range of the violin at the same level; in the works of J. J. Walther the range is raised another tone higher for practical purposes. There may also be recalled the passage from Scarlatti's *Laodicea e Berenice*, a straightforward ritornello in which the violin soars to the b‴ of the 8th position.

Now Opus V does not exceed the 3rd position for two kinds of reasons. First, from the purely instrumental point of view, the limit at which Corelli halts is that of the greatest comfort. Because of the structure of the violin, when the first finger plays the a″ of the E-string (3rd position), the balance of the left hand is perfect, and the thumb and palm find natural guiding marks as spontaneously and easily as in the 1st position. Beyond that point the element of chance begins to operate with the risk of less sure intonations and of less clear and less rich sonorities; this is the second aspect of the question, which was very probably paramount in Corelli's eyes. From all those violinists who in the course of time have invoked the Corellian tradition, we know that the *bel canto* constituted the law and the prophets. The violin, the premier instrumental upper voice, may very logically limit its ambitions to matching in compass the range of the most gifted vocal sopranos. Thus interpreted, the attitude of the pedagogue corroborates that of the artist. The one creates a fine and well-grounded technique whose foundations will bear at future times the most exuberant superstructures without yielding; the other defines an aesthetic which may be tempered, but not superseded.

Two centuries of music confirm that there is no likelihood of success in a departure from the vocal treatment of the violin. The acrobatic style of writing has its interest and always entails an intensification of suppleness to the advantage of melody. But it is not enduring; the curiosity aroused vanishes in the face of successful rivalry. Nothing is sooner vitiated than a passage of virtuosity, even in works otherwise full of music. In those compositions consisting only of "inhuman" virtuosity with intent to surprise, it follows, as a corollary, that they will fall flat once the astonishment has dissipated. To some extent Corelli himself was a victim of these laws which he so clearly perceived. His sixteenth-note *allegros* tending toward bravura, the *moto perpetuo* movements in the first sonatas of Opus V—even if they have the excuse of being excellent studies—do bore us.

It should be noted that their technical demands do not surpass those which the performance of similar *allegros* by Vitali or Torelli would call for. Nor is Corelli's boldness in the matter of double stopping without precedent. Vatielli finds, prior to 1692, prototypes of the fugal answers entrusted to the solo violin in Opus IV of Torelli, in the *Concertino per camera a violino e violoncello:*

18.

The preclassical German school goes much further: arpeggios like those in the 1st sonata of Opus V (*allegro*), chains of sixths in the 2nd (*allegro*), rapid figures in thirds in the

3rd (the first *allegro*), were current coinage with them after 1675, if not even before.

Inferior to the Germans, and indeed to the Italians, in the matter of pure technique, Corelli regains his superiority by his way of turning passages of virtuosity to good account musically and incorporating them in the weft of a piece while the majority of his rivals contented themselves with a hazardous juxtaposition. Nearer our own time, Viotti, Kreutzer, and Paganini do not demand any logical connection in their concertos between melodies and passage work, which are interchangeable without inconvenience. This is never the case with Corelli: even the cadence with which it was established usage to end sonata *allegros* has not in his works the appearance of a fortuitous accretion, as it does in the rare specimens known before his writing. Here is the cadence which concludes, with a powerful dynamic progression, the first *allegro* of the 3rd sonata, Opus V: [79]

19.

Tasto Solo

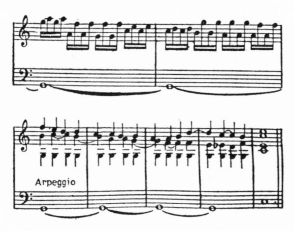

ORNAMENTATION

There remains to be considered a point about technique which affects in no less degree the profound meaning of the music: the question of ornamentation. It is known that marked differences existed between the original texts of most old works and the way their performances were envisaged in their composers' day. Although they are almost invariably underrated, a certain amount of attention is paid to those differences which relate to tempo, accents, dynamic expression, and phrasing; but a tradition is ignored whose import was very much greater because it modified the melody to the point of rendering it sometimes unrecognizable. This was the practice, inherited from the singers, of embellishing not only the *adagios* but often quick movements as well, as long as they were not written in too strict a counterpoint.

In Corelli's Opus V the aridity and even, it might be said, the poverty of certain *adagios* is difficult to understand only if the possibility of some adventitious embellishment is not kept in mind; reduced to their original outlines, those of the

3rd and 4th sonatas are so stark that it would be inconceivable to accept them as they stand. But the tradition of the composer has been preserved for us and reveals a practice of ornamentation which completely changes the appearance and character of these *adagios*.

At a date which was unascertainable with any degree of certainty until recent years, some versions appeared at Amsterdam from the presses of Pierre Mortier and Roger, in which all the *adagios* in the first part of Opus V were embroidered in the same way as Corelli was wont to play them —at least so the publishers said. Friedrich Chrysander, the first to do so, has reproduced the edition of Pierre Mortier (Augener, No. 4936, London, 1891), accompanied by a preface in which he does not seem to question the authenticity of the ornamentation. The opposite premise has also been maintained; at times it has even been alleged that Mortier's edition may have been very much later than the death of Corelli, which would have made fabrication easier.[80] But the absolutely identical edition published by Estienne Roger had surely been issued in Corelli's day. It was mentioned in the following terms in the catalogue of music appended to Volume II of a novel published in 1716—*Histoire des Sévarambes* by Denis Vairasse: "Corelli, Opera Quinta. Novelle édition gravée . . . avec les agréments marqués pour les adagio, comme M. Corelli veut qu'on les joue, *et ceux qui seront curieux de voir l'original de M. Corelli avec ses lettres écrites à ce sujet peuvent les voir chez Estienne Roger*." * The title

* Corelli, Opera Quinta. New edition engraved . . . with the ornaments for the adagios marked as M. Corelli wishes them to be played and those who are curious to see the original of M. Corelli, with his letters written on this subject, may see them at Estienne Roger's."

of the edition, as it appeared in Roger's printing, read as follows: "*Sonate a violino solo e violone o cimbalo di Arcangelo Corelli da Fusignano, Opera Quinta Parte prima.* Nouvelle Edition où l'on a joint les agréemens des Adagio de cet ouvrage, composez par M. A. Corelli, comme il les joue." *

It is known that the general practice was to publish only the schema of the *adagios*. In the same way, the harpsichordists, almost to a man, refused to reveal the ornaments of their pieces to the public. The singularity of a break with this tradition justified the precautions which the publishers ostensibly took. However great the temerity of the pirate publishers of Amsterdam may have been at that time, they certainly would never have invited public inspection and relied on bogus letters.

But the doubts that have been expressed about this (and Mario Rinaldi has gone further by "demonstrating," in a long chapter based on chronology, the unauthenticity of these ornamented editions) collapse in the light of the bibliographical discoveries of William C. Smith. Thanks to him, we know that in actual fact the ornamented edition published in London by J. Walsh and J. Hare dates not from 1720, as was long thought, but from 1711; it was announced in *The Postman* for December 11, 1711. Now, the editions of Walsh punctually reproduced the contents of those of Estienne Roger of Amsterdam. The edition involved here happens then to go back to 1710 or to the beginning of 1711; Corelli at the time was in close touch with Roger, and the ornamented edition in

---

* "Sonatas for solo violin, viola, and cembalo of Arcangelo Corelli of Fusignano. Opera Quinta Parte prima. New edition to which there has been added the ornaments of the Adagios of this work, composed by Mr. A. Corelli, and as he performs them.

question could not have been completely unknown to him. Below is an example of this interpretation of the opening *adagio* of the 3rd sonata of Opus V. If at first glance there seems something surprising about it, on reflection it corre-

20.

sponds better than the bare text of ordinary editions to the idea, passed down to us, of Corelli's suavity.

And then too, the volubility of these long garlands of sixteenth- or thirty-second-notes seems more amenable to the short and rather badly balanced bow of 1700 than do the long note-values which require more force and staying power. (We have just seen that one variation of the *follia* is especially devoted to their study.) It is certain that, so far as the *adagios* are concerned, everything was played but the written text (there are too many relevant documents to think of reproducing them). Corelli himself offers proof of this when, desiring a performance without *fioritures* for his Christmas Eve concerto (Opus VI, No. 8), he uses the indication "Arcate sostenute, e come sta,"—sostenuto bowing, and play as written.

This observation appears to contradict an assertion made in almost identical terms by Hawkins (II, 676) and by Burney (III, 555). After describing the rite which had been established in Rome of commemorating Corelli's death by an anniversary concert, the latter added: "The late Mr. Wiseman, who having arrived at Rome before the discontinuance of this laudable custom, assured me that his works used to be performed on this occasion in a slow, firm, and distinct manner just as they were written, without changing the passage in the way of embellishments. And this, it is probable, was the way in which Corelli himself used to play them."

To which the objection may be raised that the works, performed in this wise in a spacious building, were the concerti grossi (the 3rd and the 8th, according to Hawkins's text), the style of which rarely allowed extempore embroideries; in the absence of an ornamentation settled in notation, it was natural that nothing would be left to chance in a corporate performance of a solemn and devout nature.

There is no reason to advance the same doubts in respect to Opus V. This Italian ornamentation was precisely one of the points on which French criticism of this period was based: "Might it not be said, without giving offense to the votaries of Italian music, that their too frequent and ill-placed ornaments smother its expression, and that they do not at all adequately bring out the character of their works; in this resembling that Gothic architecture which, being too charged with ornaments, is obscured by them, and whence the structure of the work is no longer discernible." [81] Or again, from the same critic: "Their sonatas in two parts (that is to say, for solo violin and figured bass) ought only to be played by a solo violin, frizzing and tricking out the part as much as it pleases, and the sonatas would become very confused if the same part were performed by several instruments playing different embellishments. . . ."

A curious text of Père Castel, who in music was much more than an average amateur, confirms and explains the merits of the case for the Amsterdam edition: "It was undoubtedly only after the event that Corelli composed a separate book, which I have seen, of all the appoggiaturas, embellishments, and other variants with which he embroidered his sonatas when performing them, but which at first he was disinclined to add to his sonatas on giving them to the public. Musicians are never happy with the way their works are performed; haven't they then put their meaning down exactly?" [82]

Independently of the Amsterdam version, Nicola Matteis had published, so Quantz says, his own ornamentation of the *adagios* of Corelli. Geminiani embroidered them, too.[83] Hubert Le Blanc affirms this in his quaint way: "Geminiani made himself admired moreover in the sonatas of Corelly, which he performed. They furnished the foundation of Harmony, most able to stir and impelling into voice the sonorous instruments: Geminiani devised filling up notations of his own invention in all sorts of designs. The mind was charmed, the spirit satisfied." Furthermore, evidence has been preserved for us of Geminiani's interpretation: the conscientious Hawkins (II, 904–06), reproduces "in accordance with the manuscript" the prelude *largo* of the 9th sonata of Opus V enriched with a profusion of notes which leads to the intolerable prolixity, in this context, of Tartini and his school.

The very great interest of Geminiani's example, described

by Hawkins, lies in its not being limited to the slow movement; it also presents the *giga* and *tempo di gavotta* from the
9th sonata decorated according to the same method.

From the manner in which Tartini seized on a gavotte of
Corelli and wrote variations on it, and from the wording of a
title page such as that of Petronio Pinelli for his *Nouvelle
étude pour le violon ou manière de varier et orner une pièce
dans le goût du cantabile italien, augmentée d'une gavotte de
Corelli, travaillée et doublée par Gius. Tartini* (Paris, Boivin)
it is very doubtful whether in the ordinary way these dances
were intended to be treated rigorously. Even in compositions
of moderate dimensions, such as the sonatas and trios of Corelli
are, gavottes of eight measures in all (Opus II, the 1st trio, and
Opus V, sonata 10) have something stunted about them which
leads us to the opinion that they were repeated with variations,
like those bravura arias which singers in the theatre encored
ten or fifteen times, improvising new *fioriture* at each repeat.[84]

A new manuscript, or at least newly introduced into the
discussion, confirms this point of view. It is a little undated
work bound in red morocco; for information about it I am
indebted to Alfred Cortot. It is entitled *Correlli's Solos: grac'd
by Doburg:* the binder who distorts Corelli's name likewise
misspells that of Matthew Dubourg, one of the best violinists
of the English school. The manuscript lacks the first four
sonatas of Opus V and stops at the 11th. Nothing is more
natural than the *follia* not figuring in its contents, since this
suite of original variations by Corelli on a theme that was not
his, but common currency, was already completely decorated
and ready for performance.

The adagios in Dubourg's text are striking in the prolifera-

tion of their embroideries. Dubourg's own character is involved in this. The best known incident of his biography is
his experience at Dublin in 1742. In accompanying an aria
during one of the early performances of *The Messiah*, he
launched out into a cadenza after the last ritornello which was
so long and diffuse that he got out of his depth. He modulated
a few times before finding the right key, and when he finally
returned to it, the entire hall heard Handel, who was conducting the orchestra, say to him in his gruff voice, "Welcome
home, Mr. Dubourg."

By temperament he was an improviser. Moreover, the taste
of the age spurred him on. For one dissatisfied Handel—who
still remained his faithful friend—he found a thousand com-
placent auditors. Velocity, brilliance, and caprice were more
and more sought, and the rôle of interpreter bade fair to
eclipse that of composer.

The imprecision of Dubourg's notation indicates well
enough the freedom of a rubato which the figured bass must
be careful not to paralyze; and there is no doubt that the
figured bass could hardly accompany the violin otherwise than
by strumming chords here and there in the way it was used for
operatic recitatives: whereas the first text of Corelli and that
of Amsterdam, which was content to lightly sketch in the
austere contour of the melody, were arranged with a more
elaborated accompaniment.

Dubourg's manuscript in like manner decorates the second
part of Opus V, not limiting the process to the slow dances
and preludes; allemandes, gigues, and gavottes are freely
treated, sometimes not without irreverence, as when, for example, a gigue theme is rhythmically vitiated (sonata No. 8):

21.

and often too with an ingenuity mitigating the baldness of the model, as in the *tempo di gavotta* of the 9th sonata, where the original truly gives the impression of awaiting adornment.

22.

This question of ornaments cannot be treated exhaustively in a few pages. Special studies have invested it with profounder ramifications. Yet a considerable task remains to be accomplished in shifting the matter from the field of abstract research and translating it into practice; this amounts to our evolving a concept of the old interpretation, which is diametrically opposed to that of modern performance—the latter having for its law exactitude and a scrupulous regard for the text, the former having a latitude whose limits we are still at pains to determine. So that our appreciation of works that chronologically are quite near to us must remain circumspect, conditional, and uncertain. Corelli alone undergoes a metamorphosis by accepting the ornamentation of Amsterdam; for not only does the grandeur, austere but monotonous, of the adagios yield place to a tempered and supple quality tending toward the gracefulness of the bel canto, but this conception of the slow movements has bearing on that of the *allegros*. There can be no longer any question of inflicting on them that treatment of sabre or axe-like strokes which so often is their lot. They too become more supple, gain in deftness and variety, and turn toward a style shown us somewhat exaggerated in Dubourg's manuscript, but which, if infused with Corellian tact, may indeed be exquisite.

THE CONCERTI GROSSI, OPUS VI

It was only in December, 1712, at the very close of his life, that Corelli considered his sixth work ready for publication. It will be seen in the Bibliography (page 216) that an odd enigma is involved in the question of the publishing date; yet it in no way modifies the essence of the problem. The older he became, the more anxious was Corelli, by then a prisoner of his own fame, to offer only works of an ir-reproachable finesse to the public. His first collected works appeared with four years' space between them; five years separate Opera III and IV, there are six years between Opera IV and V; and twelve between Opus V and the concerti grossi of Opus VI.

For a long time the cognoscenti had followed the elaboration of this musical last will and testament. Adami da Bolsena in 1711 announced that "The greatest glory of the century . . . is at present occupied in bringing to perfection his sixth work of concertos, which will shortly be published and render his name for ever more immortal [sic]." [85] Already the Venetian, Giovanni Reali, in the preface to his own book of sonatas of 1709, had said that the concerti of Corelli would serve as models for the musicians of the future. Even earlier, in 1689, though it is not known whether the works alluded to were to figure in Opus VI or not, Angelo Berardi stated: "Concertos for violins and other instruments are called symphonies; those of Signor Arcangelo Corelli, the celebrated violinist, called the Bolognese, the new Orpheus of our time, are especially esteemed today." [86]

This should suffice to nullify the assertions of those who, relying on the dates of publication, see in Torelli the true creator of the genre to which Corelli is then said to have given its brilliance. But we have not yet taken account of the testimony of Georg Muffat, the most valuable witness of all, which only Andreas Moser has tried to impugn, although he was normally better inspired than this.[87] In the preface to his concertos published at Passau in 1701 (*Ausserlesener mit Ernst und Lust, gemengter Instrumental Musik. . . .*), Muffat tells us that he started to write them at Rome—where he was staying in 1682—after having heard "with astonishment some symphonies of Signor Arcangelo Corelli, which were very beautiful and very well performed by a good company of musicians." He adds: "Having noticed the great variety which this style admits of, I began to compose some of these like concertos, which I tried over with the aforesaid Signor Arcangelo Corelli, to whom I am indebted for many useful observations in respect of this collection. . . ." Muffat in his editions offers us the rare luxury of titles and prefaces in four languages—German, Italian, Latin, and French. On the basis of the German preface, Andreas Moser contended that Corelli only *directed* the performance of concertos by composers other than himself: "*producirten Concerten.*" A glance at the French text, previously referred to, would have prevented such a misunderstanding. Moser also relied on Muffat's *Armonico tributo* of 1682, a set of concertos in six parts in a mixed style—the composer authorized their performance as a trio, quartet, or whatever arrangement one fancied—in denying the existence at that date of the great prototypes of Corelli which Muffat had invoked. Yet the latter, in his 1701 collection, which this time comprised both beautiful and authentic concerti grossi, stated expressly that four of them, numbers 2, 4, 5, and 11, were written at Rome in 1682, and that numbers 10 and 12 had been commenced there.

This, it must be added, would not suffice to make Corelli the inventor of the genre. Alessandro Stradella, who died in 1682, has left us perfect models of concerti grossi in his two *Sinfonie a più Istrumenti* which are preserved in manuscript, in the Biblioteca Estense at Modena. Now, Stradella's music was familiar to the habitués of Cardinal Ottoboni's concerts, where Corelli might have formed some idea of it. As always in this kind of situation, it is no real discovery which is made just at the right moment by a single individual. We refer our reader to the *Geschichte des Instrumental-Konzerts*, by Arnold Schering: [88] he will see therein how many forerunners had contrasted, more or less consciously, a group of selected instrumentalists, the concertino, with the full orchestral mass, the concerto grosso. Deeper investigations into the history of the theater orchestra would probably assign the credit for, if not the invention of, this principle to the opera, at least in its first extensive and conscious exploitation. In the case of Stradella, or Marc Antonio Ziani, as well as many others, the symphonies which serve as overtures or entr'actes habitually employ a balance between concertino–concerto grosso. By this time it had been more than roughed out in the theater orchestrations of Lully: a number of prologues isolate the trio for flutes or oboes from the ensemble in order to set it in relief. And in 1662, in a *Serenata* for voices and orchestra composed by Dom Regio Cesti, those passages treated in the French style generally detach a concertino consisting of two violins and bass from the concerto grosso in which the viols predominate.

The position of Corelli in regard to the concerto grosso thus turns out to be identical with his position in regard to the trio and sonata. All the elements were at hand, essays in the genre had been extensively undertaken by artists of standing, the concerto grosso did exist. Let us see how he, in his turn, handled the form, and with what new luster he endowed it.

The composition of the concerti grossi extended from Corelli's maturity onward throughout his artistic life. There is nothing astonishing in the fact that they share elements and conceptions in common with the five books of trios and sonatas composed and published within the same span of time. They subdivide into two groups of which the first, the more important in this context, is comprised of the first eight concertos which correspond in spirit and nomenclature to the church trios and sonatas. The predominance of this first group is explained by the extensive use made of these concertos in religious ceremonial; not infrequently two or three were played in the course of an office. The other group is made up of the four last works assembled under a title analogous to that of the second part of Opus V: *Preludii, Allemande, Gighe, Corrente, Sarabande, Gavotte e Minuetti Parte seconda per Camera.*

The designations of the movements are the same as in the sonatas; in addition there are *minuetto* and two tempo marks, *largo andante* and *andante largo*, the former denoting a *largo* slightly more spirited, and the latter an *andante* slightly more retarded, than usual.

In the second group the four preludes are slow, the allemande and gavotte always *allegro*, the corrente and minuetto always *vivace*, the gigue *allegro* or *vivace*. This group does not consist only of dance movements; like many of the sonatas and trios it tends toward a compromise between the genres of church and chamber. Four *adagios*, of which three admittedly are only short bridge passages, an *andante largo*, and two *allegros* are to be found in the group.

The same tonalities predominate: four concertos out of the twelve are in *F* (Nos. 2, 6, 9, 12); three in *D* (1, 4, 7); two in *B*-flat (5 and 11); one in *C* (10), one in *c* (3), and one in *G* (8). In each concerto all movements, excepting the slow ones, remain in the same key. The slow movement of concertos written in the major mode is invariably in the relative minor. Of the two concertos in the minor mode, the one in *c* has its *grave* also in the minor of the subdominant *f*; the other in *g* has its central *adagio* in *E*-flat. In the 8th concerto, by way of exception with the happiest consequence, the finale (*pastorale*) which is linked to the minor common chord with which the preceding *allegro* ends, passes into the major, thus creating an impression equivalent to a mist suddenly clearing or a theater curtain rising to reveal a refulgent scene.

This tonal unity is to remain the law of the genre. Nevertheless, by 1752, Quantz will allow very much greater liberties in respect to the *adagio*, since in a concerto in C the slow movement may, in his opinion, be cast in *c, e, a, F, G,* or *g;* and a concerto in *c* may have its adagio in *E*-flat, *A*-flat, *f,* or *g.*

As far as formal planning is concerned, it is surprising that Corelli was not at all influenced by the many examples of tripartite construction (*allegro, adagio, allegro*) which the concertos of Stradella, Taglietti, and especially Torelli, offered him between 1680 and 1700, to say nothing of some sonatas of Opus III of Antonio Veracini. This arrangement, which was that of the Italian overture and was to be that of the classical symphony until the assimilation of the *scherzo,* had just the quality likely to captivate a genius smitten by fine proportions. If Corelli did not adopt this schema, perhaps it was due to his fidelity to a more fragmentary and archaic system, yet one on which the rest of his work was based; though it is surprising to note that in this connection the concertos are unprogressive in relation to the trio sonatas. Perhaps, too, there should be seen in this connection—we shall come back to the matter—the influence of operatic music, more given to dénouement and less exacting as to symmetry than the abstract symphony.

Invariably then, the concerti grossi of Opus VI have varied schemes. If we retain the designations *S* for a slow movement and *F* for a fast, and by *M* denote mixed movements that are analogous to the opening one of the first sonata of Opus V where short passages of diametrically opposed character alternate, we get the following patterns:

CONCERTO	NUMBER OF MOVEMENTS	SCHEMA
1st	6	*M S F S F F*
2nd	4	*M F S F*
3rd	5	*S F S F F*
4th	4	*F S F F*
5th	5	*F S F S F*
6th	5	*S F S F F*
7th	5	*F F S F F*
8th	6	*M S M F F S*
9th	6	*S F F F S F*
10th	6	*S F S F F F*
11th	6	*S F S S S F*
12th	5	*S F S F F*

In the writing and construction of movements, individually considered, the diversely combined influences of the former polyphony and the new homophonic style are pronounced, as is also true of the earlier works. If we only consider the *allegros,* the first concerto alone gives us a fugal *allegro* with a very sustained counterpoint (central *allegro* in C); another of homophonic conception, in which, however, the violins trace fairly close imitations (first *allegro*); and an *allegro* finale wherein the upper parts unquestionably dominate, the rest of the orchestra being reduced to a harmonic accompaniment. The strictly fugal movements evolve, as is the normal course of things, without repeats. In the other *allegros* some dispense with repeat signs, but achieve symmetry by re-exposition of the theme about the middle of the movement (the finale of the 1st concerto). Among those which are divided by a repeat sign, certain ones, such as the *vivace* of the 3rd concerto, do not at any time reintroduce the initial motif: the second repeat recalls it solely through a similarity of rhythm or scoring. Others (the finale of the 3rd concerto) begin their second repeat with the theme in the dominant key without an ultimate recapitulation in the tonic. More evolved movements (the fifth of the 6th concerto, the penultimate of the 8th) restate the theme after the intermediary development which begins after the repeat sign. Finally, in the *allegro* of the 10th concerto, we have the beginning of the theme constituting, in transposition to the dominant, the source of a development, and the entire theme recapitulated in the tonic, tonality being further affirmed by a short flourish forming a coda.

These essays at formal construction were, from all the evidence, as yet in the intuitive stage. There was no obligatory character, nothing which, by and large, might have enabled one to foresee the bonds which the future grandeur of sonata form would entail. Pertinently one might consider the strange shape of the finale of the 2nd concerto. Despite the abstract designation of *allegro*, the theme evokes the dance, and almost surely the gavotte. One expects, then, a hard and fast formal structure with repetitions of rigid periodicity. The first hearing scarcely belies these anticipations, so much do tonal logic and the symmetry with which tutti and soli are contrasted promote this illusion. On reading the score, one finds however that there is no textual recapitulation unless it be for a sort of compression in the middle of the second section where four measures juxtapose measures 1-2 and 17-18 of the first section.

In the slow movements the same diversity prevails. Some are entirely written in a fugal style; others (the first *adagio* of the 8th concerto) are in a mixed style, imitations braced with chords; others are frankly homophonic, constructed in song form A-B-A, the middle phase being either a virtually melodic passage, *e.g.* the *largo* in 3/4 meter of the 1st concerto, or a sequential development, as in the *pastorale* of the 8th concerto. Here again we must distinguish the very short *adagios*, mere bridge passages between *allegros*, of the 9th, 10th, and 11th concertos, which are in full chords in the "note against note" idiom, and the beautiful *adagios* in even eighth-notes of the 4th and the 12th concertos.

There remain the mixed movements in which *adagio* and *allegro* are integrated in a larger whole. Some have obvious symmetry: in the 8th concerto the two sections of an *adagio* of eight measures encompass an *allegro* of thirteen measures. On the other hand, sometimes the alternation of slow and fast tempi is capricious, as in certain opening phases of sonatas in Opus V. For example, the exordium of the 1st concerto is constituted thus: *Largo* (11 measures), *allegro* (8 measures), *adagio* (2 measures), *allegro* (6 measures), *adagio* (1 measure), *allegro* (8 measures), *adagio* (3 measures).

In this astonishingly flexible procedure, as in certain impressive cadential pauses or certain heroic fanfares, some people have insisted on seeing the reflection of the Venetian opera, whose overtures and instrumental interludes were often invested with a powerfully dramatic character. If a Venetian influence is probable here, there is by no means any need to postulate Corelli's staying in Venice; religious music as it was performed in the pontifical town in nowise excluded dramatic effects, antiphonal grouping, and direct allusions to the theater. The *Response faite à un curieux sur le sentiments de la musique d'Italie* by the French violinist Maugars, 1639, gives

The frontispiece to Corelli's *Sonatas for Solo Violin and Bass*, Opus V.
Rome, 1700. Dedicated to the Electress of Brandenburg, **Sophie Charlotte.**

Title page to Corelli's *Trios*, Opus III.
1689. Dedicated to Francis II, Duke
Modena.

The device of the Accademia dei Arcadia.

CONCERTI GROSSI

Con duoi Violini e Violoncello di Concertino obligati e duoi
altri Violini Viola e Basso di Concerto Grosso ad arbitrio
che si potranno radoppiare;

DEDICATI ALL'

ALTEZZA SERENISSIMA ELETTORALE
DI

GIOVANNI GUGLIELMO

PRINCIPE PALATINO DEL RENO ELETTORE e ARCI-MARESCIALLE
DEL SACRO ROMANO IMPERO DUCA DI BAVIERA GIULIERS
CLEVES BERGHE PRINCIPE DI MURS CONTE DI
VELDENTZ SPANHEIM DELLA MARCA e
RAVENSPURG SIGNORE DI
RAVENSTEIN &c &c &c

Da

ARCANGELO CORELLI DA FUSIGNANO

OPERA SESTA.

Parte Prima.

A AMSTERDAM

Chez ESTIENNE ROGER Marchand Libraire

The title page of Corelli's *C[oncerti] Grossi*, Opus VI, 1714. Dedic[ated to] the Elector Johann Wilhelm, [Count] Palatine of the Rhine. By kin[d per]mission of the Trustees of the [British] Museum.

The title page of Corelli's church sonatas, Opus I. Rome, 1681. The work is dedicated to Queen Christina of Sweden. By kind permission of the Trustees of the British Museum.

VIOLINO SECONDO

SONATE

A trè, doi Violini, e Violone, ò Arcileute
col Basso per l' Organo.

CONSECRATE

ALLA SACRA REAL MAESTÁ DI

CRISTINA ALESSANDR[A]

REGINA DI SVEZIA , &c.

DA ARCANGELO CORELLI DA FVSIGNANO,
detto il Bolognese,

OPERA PRIMA.

ROMA, Nella Stamperia di Gio: Angelo Mutij, 1681. Con licenza de S[uperiori] most circumstantial details on this subject.[89] He describes for us a musical office celebrated in the Church of the Minerva where he heard ten groups of singers, two groups being accompanied by large organs and the remaining eight groups by portable organs.

The counterpoint of the music was florid, full of beautiful melodies and a number of pleasing recitatives. Sometimes a treble of the first choir sang a recitative, then his counterpart in the third, in the fourth, and in the tenth replied. Sometimes they sang two, three, four, and five voices together from different choirs, and at other times members of every choir recited, each in turn and vying one with another. Sometimes two choirs strove against one another, then two others responded. Another time they sang an ensemble of two, three, four, or five choirs, then one, two, three, four, or five voices alone; and in the Gloria Patri all the ten choirs resumed in concert. . . . In the Antiphons, they played some excellent symphonies of one, two, or three Violins with the organ and some Archlutes playing certain airs in ballet tempo and responding to one another.

There follows an account of a concert of "Musique récitative" given at the Chapel of Saint-Marcel; after having described the oratorio, Maugars adds: "As to the Instrumental Music, it was composed of an Organ, a large Harpsichord, a Lyra Viol, two or three violins, and two or three Archlutes. Sometimes a Violin played alone with the Organ and then another answered: another time all three together played different parts, and then all the instruments took up the concert. . . ."

There may be discerned in Maugars' description that which would explain the dramatic elements of the church concerto

—agogic fluctuations derived from the recitative style, incisive rhythms of "airs in ballet tempo," contrast of soli parts and tutti. We may note in passing that, contrary to the dicta of some historians, instrumental music was no novelty in the churches of Rome when Corelli's Opus I was performed there. Maugar's letter describes in a few words not only a church trio in which according to the law of the genre two violins blend without the predominance of one over the other, but also the primitive shape of a concerto grosso, where the three soloists of the concertino (here two violins and organ) were detached first of all, after which "all the instruments took up the concert."

As to the influence of Lully, already perceptible in the sonatas and trios, it is still more marked in Opus VI. This seems clearly and easily explicable without recourse to the myth of a journey to Paris. The residence at Rome of an adherent of Lully so indoctrinated with the precepts of his master as Muffat was would suffice to account for the exchange which occurred at that time: Muffat borrowing from Corelli the best of Italian technique and reciprocally imparting his knowledge of composition in the French style.

Even more than the trios and sonatas, the concertos reflect here and there the pompous bearing, or the uninhibited gaiety of Lully's works. The *preludio* of the 9th concerto has the immediacy of a prologue of *le grand siècle*. The opening of the 3rd—a *largo* and an *allegro* built on the same motif—constitutes an authentic French overture. The *gavotta* of the 9th and the *minuetti* of the 9th and 10th proclaim their origin. But the spirit of the minuet equally animates the *vivace* movements of the 7th and 8th concertos, though they are not specifically designated as such. Likewise, the *finale* of the 2nd calls to mind a gavotte rather than the march which Arnold Schering sees in it. On the other hand the finale of the 9th and the *allegro* in 2/4 meter of the 4th are proper French marches, and this last movement is closely related to a completely Lullian finale, that by Jacques Aubert in his 3rd concerto in *A*.

In more than one passage it is less the analogy of form than the melodic or harmonic affinity which creates the bond: for example, in the *vivace* in triple meter of the 4th concerto, where the first reprise evokes the minuet, the melisma of the second is rather more reminiscent of the sarabande. More strikingly still, the 3/4 *largo* of the 1st concerto, which has a placid development with violins playing in thirds, seems meant to beguile the slumber of a hero of Marc-Antoine Charpentier or of Lully.

The orchestration is based solely on strings, plus the instruments entrusted with the figured bass. The concertino comprises two violin parts and a violoncello, the concerto grosso two violin parts, viola, and a bass part amenable to doubling. Each of the groups has its figured bass, with a harpsichord or an organ in support. (It is difficult to see by what odd notion Dr. Pepusch was constrained when, in arranging a new edition of Opus VI in London about 1730, he felt the need to transfer the viola part from the concerto grosso where Corelli had scored it to the concertino, even though in both versions the viola only plays in the tutti.)

This orchestration is less rich in changing timbres than the old Venetian symphonies or the German orchestral sonatas into which trombones and cornets enter. The number of parts, never more than four—when the concertino and concerto grosso sound simultaneously, the violin and the bass parts are common to each group, save for very rare exceptions—is exceeded in such works as the *Varie sonate*, Opus XI, of Giovanni Battista Vitali (1684), with their three violin parts, two viola parts, a violone, and figured bass.

However, at no time can Opus VI be taxed with monotony or grayness. The variety of texture to which we have briefly alluded earlier, which ranges through endless shades from strict counterpoint to the lightest woven homophony, constitutes one valuable color factor. Another, still more effective, is furnished by the orchestration in the manner in which the participations of soli and tutti are handled. The combinations are manifold; in place of the mechanical alternation of concertino and concerto grosso, we find masterly diversified treatment. In the 10th concerto, the *preludio* is conceived symphonically, with here and there a brief thinning out for a measure or half measure during which the soloists are heard without disrupting the unity of style by their virtuosity. The *allemanda* and the short *adagio* which follow are for full orchestra, and the concertino does not enter the scheme of things. The corrente is wholly assigned to the concertino, at times unaccompanied, at others accompanied with the concerto grosso deftly touched in. Then follows an *allegro* where the solo first violin predominates; here the orchestral interventions are of very variable import. Either the orchestra comes into the concertino discourse with alternate measures, or escorts it at length while scarcely allowing the embroideries of the concertino to emerge, or suppresses its own sonority into a mere obbligato role. In the concluding *minuetto* a dual symmetry prevails: an identical number of measures are given to the concertino and then repeated by the ensemble.

A final element of tone color: the treatment of the instruments of the concertino in relation to one another. In the concertos which are written in an older style, the two violins share alike in passages of equal difficulty (*allegros* of the 4th, 5th, and 7th concertos). In those whose orientation is toward the concerto for soloist, the first violin has the lion's share and reduces its partners to a mere accompanying rôle (*allegro* and *minuetto* of the 10th, and the *giga* of the 12th concertos). It also happens that the violoncello may have predominance temporarily: the first *allegro* of the 1st concerto has an exuberant bass solo in sixteenth-notes in the most brilliant register of the violoncello; the violins of the concertino emphasize it very lightly with imitative figures in eighth-notes in such manner as to set it out in full relief. The corrente of the 10th, and the allemanda of the 11th concertos proceed likewise.

So much for the written work as it is stabilized in the characters of the printed score. For it is obvious that the pleasure of the audience and the impressions of force, verve, and emotion that they might get from this music rested at least as much on the quality of the interpretation, the number and merit of the players, and the personality of the leader.

On the actual constitution of the orchestra Muffat has left us some valuable observations which have been reprinted several times in modern writings. But it would be unthinkable to forego citing them here, since, directly inspired by the example of Corelli, they aim at giving us a picture of the Roman style of performance as exact as the one Muffat had painted of the Lullian style of execution in the *Florilèges:* [90]

Concerning the Number, and the Qualities of Musicians and of Instruments

I. Not having a large number of Violins, or wishing to hear these Concertos only with a few instruments, you could form a perfect Trio, which is always the Principal and necessary group, by selecting the trio parts entitled Violino Primo Concertino, Violino Secondo Concertino and Basso continuo et Violoncino Concertino, and preferably using a small French bass rather than the double or large bass which is called a Violone: to which you can add a Harpsichord or a Theorbo, or other similar instrument which would play the same part as the small French bass referred to. And then have a care that all play loudly at the sign *T* or Tutti, and softly or tenderly at the sign *S* or Solo. In addition, look to the exact observation of loud and soft under the expressions forte and piano, or under the simple letters *f* and *p* which mean the same thing.

II. Adding to the aforementioned parts that of the Viola Prima, you would have a quartet ensemble, and a quintet by again adding to this the Viola Seconda.

III. To these five parts then join the three residual Violino Primo Concerto grosso, Violino Secondo Concerto grosso, and Violone, o Cembalo Concerto Grosso, if a greater number of players enables you to do this. Have each of these parts played simply by a single instrument, or more sonorously by two or three together, accordingly as the number of available players and reason dictate. And, in that case, so as to invest the bass of the large choir with greater majesty, you could well use the double Bass, which the Italians call the Contrebasse or Violone.

IV. Having a still greater number of players, you could reinforce not only the first or second upper parts, or Violins, of the large choir, signified by the words *Concerto grosso;* but also the one or another of the tenor or inner Viola parts, as well as the bass of aforesaid large choir, which you could further elaborate with the accompaniment of Harpsichords, Theorbos, Harps, or other similar instruments as you might deem suitable; nevertheless leave the three parts of the little choir, or principal Trio (Concertino) to be played singly as to number, but elegantly as to the manner of playing by the three best members of your band, accompanying them by a single Harpsichord or Theorbo, and doubling each part by an additional Violin only when performing in some very spacious place and when the large choir is extremely numerous. I leave to your judgment the reinforcing of the principal parts of the large choir, such as the first and second violins (Concerto grosso), as well as the middle parts; likewise your properly elaborating the bass of the large choir (Violone, e Cembalo Concerto Grosso) with as many small as large, or double, basses and other Instruments such as bassoons, Bombardes, and accompaniments of Harpsichords, Theorbos, Harps, or Regals.

If among your Musicians you have some accomplished oboe players, you could successfully arrange for the three parts of your Trio, or little choir (Concertino) to be played by two Oboes and a Bassoon in many of these Concertos; or at least some of their airs chosen for this purpose, being attentive to choosing those in keys, or transposing them into keys, suitable for these instruments, or raising them an octave or altering short passages which lie beyond the instruments' ranges. It is thus that I had the First [of Muffat's own concertos], the Third, the Ninth, and the Tenth played in their actual keys; and the Seventh by transposing it from the key of *E* to *E*-flat, with the necessary changes. And this shall suffice for the number and qualities of Musicians and of Instruments.

It is seen that the effective strength of the orchestra was eminently variable, depending on the means at one's disposal, the spaciousness of the rooms, and the ostentation of the ceremony. This flexibility has an element of surprise for us for much the same reason that we are surprised at the toleration of Couperin or Rameau in the matter of performance. We know at all events the numerical extent of the augmentation of the orchestra at times of great solemnities. Yet generally speaking it reached the number of musicians which is that of our modern "chamber orchestras." Arnold Schering mentions a concerto of Torelli, preserved in the archives of San Petronio at Bologna, which comprises thirty-seven band parts, several of which could in fact be used by two performers. At times these figures were considerably exceeded. For certain festivities at San Petronio in 1716 there were 123 musicians and extra singers.[91] In 1722, a traveler, Edward Wright, counted in the same church a total of 140 performers.[92] In 1740 Charles de Brosses estimated there were two hundred instrumentalists assembled in the papal chamber at Monte Cavallo for the sacred concert on Christmas Eve.[93] So far as Corelli is concerned, we know that he was appointed to direct an ensemble of 150 strings at the time of the festivities organized by Christina of Sweden in 1687 in honor of Pope Innocent XI.[94]

Corelli's ability as leader of the orchestra was universally acknowledged. Muffat rendered homage to him; so did Crescimbeni in his account of a fête at the *Accademia dei Arcadi*, wherein he states that Corelli "began the musical revels, conducting one of the magnificent symphonies composed at the abode of Cardinal Ottoboni," and that "the perfect intonation as between wind instruments and strings was marvellous." A passage from the *Ferragosto* of Zappi and Crescimbeni extols Corelli's mastery fulsomely:

Now do you not see him, who with his right hand, as though it were wingèd, gently directs the celestial choir? He is his own peer, and equalled by no other. Already he has assisted the melodies of the Angelic Hosts; then to make earth more blessed he has forsaken the heavenly choir and come to us, bringing with him from his bright mansion a unison never yet heard on earth, so that we take a hundred instruments for one.[95]

If we can rely on Burney's testimony, a judge who was qualified in another sphere greatly admired Corelli's art as a leader: "At the time of Corelli's greatest reputation," wrote Burney (III, 557—note that the passage was plagiarized word for word by Burgh in *Anecdotes of Music*, II, 267, and by Dubourg in *The Violin*, p. 43) "Geminiani asked Scarlatti what he thought of him; who answered, that he found nothing greatly to admire in his composition, but was extremely struck by the manner in which he played his concertos and the nice management of his band, the uncommon accuracy of whose performance gave the concertos an amazing effect to the eye as well as to the ear. For," continued Geminiani, "Corelli regarded it as essential to the ensemble of the band that their bows should all move exactly together, all up, all down; so that at his rehearsals, which constantly preceded every public performance of his concertos, he would immediately stop the band if he discovered one irregular bow."

It seems that this discipline was maintained at the time of the ceremony which took place each year at the Pantheon to commemorate the anniversary of Corelli's death, in the course of which rite some of the concerti grossi of Opus VI were played. (See above, page 114.) Thus, from what has been said it can be surmised that the concerti grossi escaped the profuse ornamentation to which the trios and sonatas were sub-

jected; but this cannot be either invariably or infallibly asserted, since, as we have seen, Corelli believed that in order
to get long note-values without embroideries in the *grave*
of the 8th concerto, he had to specifically request *Arcate
sostenute e come stà*—play sostenuto and as it stands.[96]
Alternatively, when the case arose, he indicated the embellishments he desired with adequate clarity. For instance,
the end of the second repeat and coda of the sarabande of
the 11th concerto:

By virtue of this precision, this character of finality in the
writing, Opus VI is the most modern of his works despite
its ties with the old polyphony. But its novelty goes further,
and also—though there is no question of any causal relation-
ship involved—its artistic merit. In spite of being written in
a more scored style of composition which renders more
seductive the contrivance of mechanically and perfunctorily
wrought sequences and syncopated imitations, we find in
Opus VI, on the contrary, the refinement of such passages.
The sequences abound only in the violinistic writing, from
whence derives a vitality, a sprightliness to which Opera I to
V never attained, or at least not to such a degree. There is
also unwonted vigor, and an insistence on tonality equal to

Vivaldi in the first *allegro* of the 7th concerto, which is a veritable pendant in *D* to Vivaldi's D Minor Concerto for two violins in *L'Estro Armonico;* in this Opus VI, are also to be found cantilena passages of an accent hitherto unheard in the music of Corelli. I refer to the *andante largo*, pensive and suave, of the 7th concerto; to the luminous *pastorale* of the 8th; and above all to the fugal *grave* of the 3rd, with its pathetic intervals of fourths, fifths, and diminished sevenths, its octave leaps which halt on a tied note and are followed by a strain which descends as though discouraged. Here, into the old polyphonic form, steals a feeling of anguish which might be described as romantic had not, at all times and long before the era of romanticism, such masters as Josquin des Prés, Froberger, and Bach given powerful expression to it.

It is not easy to understand the contempt which Scarlatti is supposed to have shown toward the concertos; and Burney's remarks should be treated with prudent reserve. Invariably, Corelli's contemporaries and the immediately following generations made a great fuss over Opus VI, as will be seen in the next chapter. Burney, expressing his own conviction, wrote at the end of the eighteenth century: "The Concertos of Corelli seem to have withstood all the attacks of time and fashion with more firmness than any of his other works. The harmony is so pure, so rich, and so grateful; the parts are so clearly, judiciously, and ingeniously disposed; and the effect of the whole, from a large band, so majestic, solemn, and sublime that they preclude criticism and make us forget that there is any other music of the same kind existing" (III, 556–57).

III

Corelli's Influence

THE INFLUENCE of Corelli on the development of his art has been considerable. It has been exerted in many ways: by the violinist's direct example and teaching, by the diffusion of his works, by the controversies to which they have given rise. Corelli became more than a master in foreign eyes: he was the symbol of Italianism, and its banner.

Among his direct disciples the most notable were Francesco Gasparini (master in his turn of Pugnani and Giardini, and particularly known as the author of *Armonico practico al cimbalo*) and Locatelli. When Walsh and Hare published a collected edition of the first four works of Corelli at London in September, 1705, Gasparini, in a statement to *The Postman* dated September 29, 1705, attested his having corrected the edition and guaranteed its accuracy, as "an intimate friend of the composer and one fully cognisant with his activities, having been a pupil of Corelli for six years" (W. C. Smith, *op. cit.*, p. 58). Locatelli, one of the propagators of the concerto grosso after Corelli, was less influenced as a virtuoso—he was very young at the time of the master's death—yet he was always loyal to Corelli's memory, judging from the droll and yet precise account imparted to us by the historian

Blainville. Discoursing on the sensitivity of birds to music, he observed their pleasure at hearing instruments, "so much so that Locatelli, with the first *adagio* of the fourth sonata of Corelli, was certain by his manner of playing to make a canary, in a transport of delight, fall from his perch in the cage." [97] Other pupils were Pietro Castrucci, Stefano Carbonelli, and Francesco Geminiani, all three of whom made careers in England, and Michele Mascitti, a Neapolitan who went to Paris where Baptiste Anet was promoting the "vogue" for Corelli. Much ado was made of the reception which this Frenchman had received from the master: "He singularly loved the works of Corelli," wrote the Abbé Pluche, "and had so delicately caught their flavor, that having played them in Rome before Corelli himself, this great musician tenderly embraced him and presented him with his bow"; [98] and an anonymous writer in the *Mercure de France* of August, 1738, said: "Anet already had a prodigious technique when he arrived at Rome; Corelly himself was surprised at this, and was delighted to show him how to perform the sonatas in his way." According to Lecerf de la Viéville, Anet is supposed to have had "three or four years of study under Corelli" (III, 320).

Some historians, including Fétis and Wasielewski, also mention Carlo Tessarini of Rimini; but this is only conjecture. As for Pisendel, whom E. Heron Allen [99] makes out to be a pupil of Corelli, the error is obviously derived from Johann Adam Hiller, who reproduced Printz's confusion between Corelli and Torelli. Still another German, Johann Georg Christian Störl, widely known as an organist and composer, tells us that about 1703 he had the benefit of

Corelli's advice in Rome. (See his autobiography, printed by Mattheson.) A famous Spanish violinist, José Herrando, was said also to have been his pupil; where or when is not known, and it must be admitted that this is hardly likely. On the one hand, no trace has been found in Herrando's *Arte y puntual Explicacion del modo de tocar el Violin*, now in the Biblioteca Nacional of Madrid, of the assertion which R. Mitjana [100] claimed to have discovered therein: "In the introduction to his technical work, he declares he had lessons from Corelli." On the other hand, this method was published in 1757 (engraved at Paris the previous year), and the other known works of Herrando are all subsequent to 1750. Finally, Woldemar, in his republication of Leopold Mozart's *Violinschule*, refers (p. 68) to "Principles of Arpeggio by Herrando of Madrid, a pupil of Christiani." But Christiani, a violinist at the court of Prince Ferdinand of Prussia, was born in 1722.

We are certainly far from knowing all those who might have had lessons from Corelli, whose worldly position was as brilliant as his ascendancy over professional artists was great. The Honourable Roger North in his *Memoirs of Musick* observed with some irony that "most of the nobility and gentry that have travelled in Italy affected to learn of Corelli." Few of these English names have come down to us: however, we would mention Lord Edgecumbe, on whose commission the painter Hugh Howard, while a guest of Cardinal Ottoboni, is said to have painted the magnificent portrait of Corelli that has been popularized by Smith's engraving.[101] A set of sonatas preserved in Vienna carries as the designation of their composer the inscription L. D. I. M. S. *Inglese allievo d'Arcangelo Corelli* (L. D. I. M. S. English pupil of Arcangelo

Corelli); L(or)D or L(a)D(y) I. M. S. was very probably a dilettante, for a professional composer would have had no reason to remain anonymous.

From a purely didactic point of view, Corelli's influence has been profound and lasting. Not only the violin methods, such as those of Geminiani and Tessarini, are based on his principles; but, according to Burney, "Tartini formed all his scholars on these solos (Opus V)." [102] And, he adds, "Signor Giardini has told me that of any two pupils of equal age and disposition, if the one were to begin his studies by Corelli, and the other by Geminiani, or any other eminent master whatever, he is sure that the first pupil would become the best performer." In his treatise *Dell' origine e delle regole della Musica*, Dom Antonio Eximeno, extolling the merits of Corelli, who "at the beginning of the century brought instrumental music to its point of perfection," praised in the works "the variety of beautiful and well worked out [fugal] subjects, the exact observance of the laws of harmony, the firmness of the basses, *the fitness for exercising the hands of the performer*." Galeazzi, who was truly the most reflective of pedagogues, in 1791 still advocated the daily study of Opus V: performers of a certain attainment should start at the outset with the second part; then, by themselves, afterwards go on to the first part, which will reveal to them "the arcana of the art." He expressly recommended as bowing exercise the *allegros* in sixteenth-notes of the first, third, and sixth sonatas.[103]

This pedagogic quality must be appreciated, certainly. But we are indebted to Corelli for something far greater and better. If, throughout the history of music for the violin, there be conceded the coexistence of two tendencies, one intrinsically musical, the other oriented toward acrobatic technique, everything which pertains to the first evolves within Corelli's sphere. Before Tartini's *per ben suonare, bisogna ben cantare* (to play well one must sing well), it was Corelli himself who made his pupils attentive right from the start to the vocal quality of the sonority of the violin: "*Non lo udite parlare?*" (Don't you hear it speak?) [104]

This submission to the model of the human voice had also been made, either by instinct or deliberate intent, by predecessors and by rivals such as Bassani and Torelli. It only acquired the force of law because of the personal ascendancy of Corelli. He alone called the necessary halt at the point when the chaotic and fortuitous discoveries of undeveloped virtuosity ran the risk of giving free rein to charlatanism.

Simple as it was, his discipline guaranteed the future of the violin. Not only did the direct inheritors of Corelli—Somis, Pugnani, Viotti, and, stemming from them, the modern Franco-Belgian School—obey it, but also the classic composers, Nardini, Tartini, Leclair, and Benda. Undoubtedly the initiator had to be surpassed, and the bounds that he had set were to be extended considerably: an Agujari soars over the limits of other sopranos. But with rare exceptions, Corelli's principles prevailed. Beneath the most audacious passages, the breaths and the inflections of the voice will be recognized; and, according to the times, this will constitute the force or the frailty of the violin in the public taste. In Corelli's day, and for a long time afterward, this was its force; in point of fact, this great directive principle was being diffused at that time through far vaster domains than Corelli's. The modernist movement, which in the earliest years of the eighteenth century was so clearly adumbrated by the operas of Reinhard Kaiser of Hamburg, and propagated by Mattheson and by Telemann, was to substitute the contemporary regime for the former dominion of counterpoint; this movement had for its slogan: "Whatever piece is written, whether it be vocal or instrumental, must be singable." This endeavor to free the beautiful melodic line was truly one which the composer of Opus V worked for indefatigably. Yet not with the same objectives? Surely he was not assigned the task of destroying an established order; surely he only wished to strengthen, discipline, and ennoble the playing of the instrument which he preferred? Perhaps so. But the new spirit which was in the air and was to manifest itself at so many other points of musical Europe pervaded Corelli's last works, though unperceived by him. By this token, counterpoint becomes less tyrannical, progressions less predictable, the upper voice assumes some independence, the style acquires an immediacy at first beneficial before becoming a bane. We have some difficulty in being sensible of these differences, blurred as they are by the remoteness of time. His contemporaries were sensitive to them. The most violent of Corelli's detractors, Lecerf de la Viéville, blamed him for abandoning the academic formulae of the older art: "They both [Corelli and Buononcini] write few fugues, countersubjects, and ground basses—frequent beauties in other Italian works!" [105] To be fair, there should be grouped with Corelli the violinists of Rome, Bologna, and Venice who worked in the same vein and reinforced his activity. A volume would not suffice for this, as it would raise, *inter alia*, the question of the entire history of the symphony before the Mannheim School.

Turning to what is definite, we will take into account some facts evidential of the diffusion of Corelli's works in the eighteenth century.

To begin with, Italy. It is scarcely surprising to discover that the great Vivaldi, Corelli's veritable antithesis in the masterpieces of his maturity, began by imitating him almost to the point of servility. He undoubtedly became familiar with Corelli's work primarily through Francesco Gasparini, a pupil of Arcangelo, who in 1708 and perhaps earlier was Vivaldi's colleague at the Pietà. Not only does Opus I of the *Red Priest* end with a *follia* imitating that of Opus V, but the *caprice* of his 1st sonata is based exactly on the harmonic scheme of the Corellian *follia*, transposed into *g*; practically the same thing occurs in the *preludio* in the 8th sonata. The *preludio* of the 7th is an artless imitation of the celebrated gavotte in F of Opus V, slackened to *largo* pace, and transposed in *E*-flat:

24.

etc

An equally pointed reminiscence is to be found in Vivaldi's Opus II of 1709 in the allemande of the 4th sonata:

25.

More than one affinity also exists between the melodic contours of the slow movements. This will prevail up to and in Opus III, the celebrated *Estro Armonico*, where the *largo* of the 12th concerto opens with a motif which is exactly superimposable on the *grave* of the 6th sonata of Corelli:

26.

Finally, several passages in double stopping, particularly one in a concerto in manuscript possessed by the Landes-bibliothek at Dresden (Cx. 1705), are similar to the most intricate "fugues" of Opus V by virtue of the spareness and brevity of their themes, which are often repeated in symmetrical progressions. It must in fairness be conceded that Corelli himself could have discovered the model for this writing in certain German primitives, or in some of his compatriots, such as Il Gobbo.

Let us deliberately pass over Corelli's pupils, such as Mossi and Mascitti, avowed and conscious imitators whose early works abound in allusions to the style of their master. It is, however, curious to find in the work of Gasparini in two *allegros*—one from a concerto, the other from a symphony (Nationalbibliothek, Vienna, Nos. 124 and 125)—themes through which one gets a glimpse of the gavotte in *F*. In those times this gavotte seems to have obsessed all those engaged in musical composition. Albinoni, in whose works other traces of Corellian influence are found, especially in the slow movements, built the middle phase of an *allegro* on its theme:

27.

Now, this *allegro* is part of the second concerto from his Opus II, published at Venice in 1700; the beginning of this same year had seen the appearance of Corelli's Opus V. The first concerto of Albinoni's collection contains an *allegro assai* which opens with the harmonic scheme of this gavotte in its original key of *F*. There are other Corellian traits in this Opus II; for example, in the *largo* of the second sonata. As for the concertos (Albinoni had composed this Opus II with alternate sonatas and concertos), R. Giazotto, *Tomaso Albinoni*, p. 115, believes that Albinoni was in a position to have heard the concerti grossi of Corelli which were published first in 1714 but which were often performed in Rome after 1685. And a brother of Albinoni was a page in the service of Anna Maria Ottoboni, mother of Cardinal Pietro Ottoboni, Corelli's patron. Even Tartini, who openly takes the gavotte as the theme of his variations in the *Art of Bowing*, writes a *largo* in his Opus IV (5th sonata) which is a sort of melodic amplification of it: [106]

28.

Moreover, Dr. Burney claimed, not without plausibility, that Tartini used to make a complete act of submission to him whose disciple he never had the good fortune to be: "He was so ambitious of being thought a follower of Corelli's precepts and principles, that after his own reputation was at its zenith, he refused to teach any other music to his disciples, till they had studied the *Opera Quinta*, or Solo's, of Corelli" (III, 562).

Giuseppe Valenti utilized a corrente from the fourth book of Corelli's trios in one of his *Sinfonie a tre* of 1701, and he entitled the seventh sonata of his own Opus V *La Corelli*. Giovanni Battista Reali, a Venetian, dedicated to the master, "il Columbo della Musica" his *Sonate e Capricci . . . con una Follia* (Opus I, Venice, 1709). Giovanni Battista Tibaldi composed a *Svario* [variation] *ō Capriccio di otto battute a l'imitatione del Corelli* (Amsterdam, 1704).

It is probable that Francesco Bonporti was directly or indirectly a pupil of Corelli. Guglielmo Barblan has established that beginning October 30, 1691, and for some time thereafter, Bonporti was enrolled in the German College at Rome, where Matteo Fornari taught; Fornari was the intimate friend to whom Arcangelo entrusted the publication of his Opus VI. It is therefore quite possible that Corelli supervised Bonporti's instruction.

Should we consider the benefit which Scarlatti derived from his long acquaintance with Corelli? Dent finds an obvious example in the mastery of the violin writing in the *Serenades*, some of which were written about 1706, others about 1720.[107] Perhaps it is a question of greater or lesser adaptation: the previous scores of Scarlatti betray no inexperience with respect to the treatment of bowed instruments, and the anecdote of *Laodicea e Berenice*, if the story is true, is found to cut both ways.

Burney, without additional proof (III, 557), claims to find in the *adagio* of the 8th concerto of Corelli a borrowing from a cantata of Scarlatti's which dates from 1704. Nothing is less certain: the resemblance is based on two measures of an extremely ordinary theme (3rd and 4th measures, marked *adagio*); and Corelli's concerto, published in Opus VI in 1714, was quite probably written before 1704.

I do not know the sonatas of Padre Martini, two books "which were published one in Amsterdam and the other in Bologna in 1752" according to Fayolle,[108] and which "he avows" had been modeled on Corelli's Opus III. But Porpora, in his *XII Sonate per Violino e Basso*, published in Vienna in 1754, links them directly to the style of Opus V.

Again, these notes cannot pretend to be complete; after all, for a long time in Italy the four books of trios and Opus V were the daily bread of theorists and virtuosos. As for the concerti grossi, here is a fragment of a letter from Charles de Brosses written at the end of 1739: "They [the sons of James III, the Pretender] give an exquisite concert every week; it is the best music in Rome; I never miss it. Yesterday I entered while they were performing the famous concerto of Corelli called *La Notte di Natale;* I confessed my regret at not having arrived earlier to hear the whole work. When it was finished and they wanted to pass on to another piece, the Prince of Wales said: 'No, wait, let us begin this concerto again; I have just heard it said by Monsieur de Brosses that he would be very gratified to hear it right through.' " [109]

Corelli's influence in Germany at the beginning diffused less on the surface than in the depth. It has been seen earlier to what extent Georg Muffat was imbued by it. His *Armonico Tributo* of 1682, his concerti grossi of 1701, are as much a tribute to the Italian master as to Lully. Professor Bukofzer (*op. cit.*, p. 262) has stressed the degree to which the organist Jan Reinken of Hamburg, in his *Hortus musicus* (1687), Dietrich Buxtehude in his *Sonates à trois* (1696), Fux, Fasch, and Graupner were indebted to Corelli—Bach showed a special fondness for the works of Graupner. Corelli's work was familiar also to the principal theorist of the then modern movement, Mattheson,[110] as well as to its most conspicuous champion, Telemann, who wrote *Les Corelizantes* and, in his autobiography, declared that he was at first "given as models the pieces of Steffani, Rosenmüller, Corelli, and Caldara." Among the other biographies also collected by Mattheson, only two mention Corelli, that of Störl, his pupil at Rome, and that of Christophe Raupach. In the organ works of Johann Gottfried Walther, a composer and a lexicographer, and consequently inquisitive by vocation, there is to be found a transcription *variée* of a prelude from Opus V (11th sonata).

In truth these few "debtors" of Corelli are of little importance in contrast with the two giants Bach and Handel, both to some extent beholden to him. An indefatigable reader, of boundless musical curiosity, Bach was acquainted before 1715 with the important works of Albinoni, Legrenzi, and Corelli, not to mention the early works of Vivaldi. As for Corelli, the quotation already referred to of a fugal subject taken from Opus III has, perhaps, the significance of an act of esteem: in any case it reveals an interest and an accurate recollection. This is so with respect to many features, not only of scoring, but of melody and rhythm: the broken chord figurations of the Bach's violin concertos have the form and same rigidity of those to be met with, for example, in the *presto* of the 4th trio of Opus III; a design, corresponding note for note with the opening of the fugue in the *Choral Prelude and Fugue* of César Franck, and which Bach used habitually, is already present in an *allegro* of the 11th trio of Corelli's Opus I. It would be inappropriate at this stage to dilate on other similarities of detail. In each case Bach's intervention reveals itself by an enlargement and maturation of the borrowed material, which acquires the hallmark of original creation. Likewise with regard to form: the sonatas and several of the Brandenburg Concertos continued the evolution already in progress in Corelli's Opus V and VI, an evolution which, as we know, was neither initiated by him nor, at this elementary stage, nourished by his contribution alone. But Corelli's dignified mastery and his authority earned him the merit of passing on to Bach the finest expression of a certain tendency of Italian instrumental music; the other tendency, more modern, more lyrical, being represented—and with what distinction—by the concertos of Vivaldi.

As for Handel, he never scrupled to borrow from one whom, it is said, he taxed with avarice. During his youthful studies at Halle, his master Zachow who, like Bach, had gathered together an important collection of works by foreign masters, set Handel to compose in their various styles. Corelli was one of these models; and the "dear Saxon" in his own hand copied extracts from Corelli's works. Not only Handel's *Concerti Grossi* of 1740 testify to the profit which he was able to derive from them, but so do several passages from his great vocal compositions, such as the chorus from *Esther*, which Chrysander mentions, which reproduces an ostinato design from the 12th concerto of Opus VI in an amplified form. Regarding the anecdote of Corelli's coming to grief over a sight reading of the French overture to *Il Trionfo del Tempo* (1707), it is to be noted that Handel replaced this overture by a concerto grosso "employing in it the typical formulas and mannerisms of Corelli to such a degree that the whole could be taken for a calculated parody of the Corelli style, were it not for the pathetic slow movement that only Handel could write" (Bukofzer, p. 321).

In Handel's sonatas for two violins and bass, several themes seem reminiscences of Opus III and Opus V.[111] But one should be wary of asserting this. For the sake of curiosity and, perhaps, as an appeal to prudence too, lovers of this type of coincidence should be reminded of the presence of a characteristic formula used by Corelli with the same emphasis and almost the same technique in the *ciacona* of his Opus II, in the *vivace* of his 3rd trio, Opus III, and in the trio in D, No. 1, Opus 70 by Beethoven, who hardly gave a thought to imitating:

29.

To revert to the period which most interests us. Even granted the few decades during which Corelli's work retained its vivifying power, it does not seem that the public of Germany, which was admittedly in high degree separatist, paid much attention to him at that time. His light did not shine beyond a few professional circles, or, as far as a prince's court was concerned, beyond that of the Rhine Palatinate.

England reacted quite differently for various reasons, two of which are easily distinguishable. One was the English craze for the violin and all Italian music, which in Corelli's lifetime brought about an influx of virtuosi, several of whom were among his best pupils, to London; the other was the activity of London publishers who were as prompt as Mortier, Roger, or Le Cène of Amsterdam to reproduce, legally or otherwise, the impressions printed at Rome, Bologna, or Venice.[112]

From the middle of the seventeenth century, and despite the avowed xenophobia of official musicians like Matthew

Locke or John Playford,[113] imitation of the foreigner had
caused a spate of English sonatas: in 1653 those which William
Young produced at Innsbruck where he was in service at the
court of the Grand Duke Ferdinand, in 1660 those of John
Jenkins, which were actually printed in London.

A violin school sprang up, in the face of which the violists
little by little gave ground—these for a long time had been
the exclusive favorites of the *mélomanes* and were possessed
of an abundant repertoire furnished by the best composers
of the kingdom. The English violinists—Davis Mell, Paul
Wheeler, George Hudson, the elder John Banister, and Stagins
—began to enjoy a measure of prestige. The advent in 1656
of the brilliant Baltzar [114] from Lübeck lowered them a little
in the public's esteem. They again lost ground, but without
any detriment to the vogue of their instrument, when Charles
II resolved in 1666 to install French music at his court. The
cult of Italian music benefitted greatly from this, for the taste
of the king was not so much favorable to the French style as
opposed in principle to the old English style, so that musicians
from beyond the Alps followed without difficulty in the wake
of Grabu and his violins. A very great master, Nicola Matteis,
appeared in London in 1672 and created a sensation there. The
Honourable Roger North [115] praised the subtlety of his bowing as being without parallel, as well as his exquisite compositions. According to Burney (IV, 640) it was Matteis who
"polished and refined our ears and made them fit and eager for
the sonatas of Corelli."

Meanwhile, concerts were being organized; those of John
Banister in 1673, of Thomas Britton in 1678, of Sadler in
1683, at which Italian music was the principal attraction. The

best society at that time, says North, went in for the "consorts" (all ensemble works) of Cazzati and Vitali, while the
old fancies for viols were left to provincial amateurs.

Corelli had only to join in to be victorious. The diffusion
of his work began in 1695, and continued with ever-quicken-
ing rhythm for more than a quarter of a century. On the 23rd
of September, 1695, there appeared in the *London Gazette*
the following advertisement: "Twelve Sonatas (newly come
over from Rome) in three parts, composed by Signeur Archangelo Corelli, and dedicated to His Highness the Elector of
Bavaria, this present year 1694, are to be had fairly prick'd
from the true original at Mr. Ralph Agutter's, Musical Instrument Maker, over against York Buildings in the Strand, London." Van der Straeten, who quotes this announcement, observes that this is a pirated edition, the first legitimate copy
being that of Walsh about 1710.

But what this collection, dedicated to His Highness the
Elector of Bavaria in 1695, can be is an open question.

As for Opus V, the violinist John Banister, Junior introduced it in London the very year of its publication. A notice
in the *London Gazette* (the issue for the 8th to 11th of July,
1700) announces that subscribers could get copies of it, "being
now brought from Rome," on the following Monday at Mr.
Banister's or at Mr. King's (Robert King, a member of the
King's band). Six weeks later the same periodical (issue for
the 26th to 29th of August) draws attention to a reprint of
the same set "being much fairer and more correct in the
Musick, than that of Amsterdam," by John Walsh, who had
not lost any time, and who, because of the success of this
enterprise, was to undertake a few years later the engraving

of Corelli's earlier work, then the concertos, and then the collected edition of the six books.[116]

The discovery of Opus V had been the work of a violinist, John Banister. Another violinist, Henry Needler, launched the concertos. A consummate musician, very much esteemed in fashionable circles, he was considered one of the best interpreters of Corelli. One day a bookseller of the Strand named Prévost received, in a batch of books consigned to him from Amsterdam, Opus VI, which had quite recently appeared (1715). His first thought was to take it to Needler. The virtuoso was not at home, but at the weekly concert given at the house of J. B. Loeillet. Prévost forthwith betook himself to the latter's house. Such was the enthusiasm of Needler, Loeillet, and their colleagues, so the story has it, that they played the whole twelve concertos through without rising once from their seats.

The historian Henry Davey, and others after him, attributed the distinction of having first publicly performed a sonata of Opus V in England to a somewhat obscure artist, Thomas Deane, in 1709. But it is scarcely probable that Banister and Needler would have left the matter in his hands. Besides, the Italians living in London, such as Matteis, would not be averse to welcoming anything sensational which might appear among them. In any case it must be taken as practically certain that Gasparini, a pupil and passionate admirer of Corelli, who was often to be heard at York Buildings from 1702 to 1704, would not miss any suitable opportunity to render homage to his master in a way reflecting credit on himself.

At this time the popularity of Corelli in London attained surprising proportions. Long before practical familiarity with his works could have gained him justifiable goodwill, his name already symbolized there the musical genius of his race. The first trios of Purcell are particularly influenced by the recollection of G. B. Vitali and Nicola Matteis: but the poet, Thomas Brown, in 1693, adjudged them otherwise, as witness these lines printed in the second book of the *Harmonia Sacra* by Henry Playford:

> In thy productions we with wonder find
> Bassani's genius to Corelli's joined.

It is not a sheer impossibility that some compatriot of Purcell, on returning from Italy about 1681, may have showed him an original or copy of Corelli's Opus I, and that Purcell may have been inspired by them in his twelve trio sonatas of 1683, the only instrumental collection to which Brown could be alluding. This being so, one is surprised, when reading these sonatas, that a musician such as Purcell should have reaped so little profit from his model, and have continued to use an archaic and gauche style of violin writing to the point of obscuring in part the sonatas' science and expressive beauty.

Shortly afterward Ravenscroft, in his Opus I published in Rome, 1695, contrived to ape Corelli. An apothecary named Sherard published at Amsterdam two sets of sonatas, the first dated before 1702; according to Hawkins (II, 678), any listener not forewarned would have attributed them to the great Italian. The second part of the *Division Violin*, 4th edition, was announced by *The Post Man* (April 14, 1705) as containing "several solos of Arcangelo Corelli."

The same year and in the same periodical a controversy

started between Walsh and Hare, who had announced the publication of the first four works of Corelli in a new edition carefully corrected by "the ingenious Signior Nicolini Haiam," and the same Nicolini Haym who asserted that he had neither directly nor indirectly corrected this edition; but that he had given his attention to the edition which Stephen Roger [Estienne Roger] of Amsterdam had prepared.

J. Walsh, Randall, and J. Hare announce in 1709 "Six Sonata's . . . composed in imitation of Arcangelo Corelli by Wm Topham, Opera Terza" in the *Daily Courant* for November 14, 1709.

This is really fame with its inexorable price: the French polemist Lecerf de la Viéville in 1706 charged the English with having written "by now, sonatas and yet more sonatas, more difficult and more fantastic than those of Opus V of Corelli." [117]

A little later Ned Ward composed a burlesque poem on the concerts of Britton, wherein an habitué of the concerts declared:

> We Thrum fam'd Corella's Aires;
> Fine Solos and Sonnettos. [118]

Another poem, quoted in the *Great Abuse of Musick* by the Reverend Arthur Bedford (1711), protested against the abuse of "sad Sonatas" and continues:

> Well were it if our Wits would lay Embargo's
> On such Allegros and such Poco Largos;
> And would enact it, there presum not any
> To teize Corelli, or burlesque Bassiani,

And with Divisions and ungainly Graces,
Eclipse good sense, as weighty Wigs do Faces;

A futile attack. Success was such that certain musicians, among them Thomas Shuttleworth, earned their daily bread by copying Opera I to IV, the first editions of which had been printed with the old lozenge-shaped notes which made reading difficult (Hawkins, II, 675).

The arrival of Corelli's best pupils intensified the movement. After Gasparini came Geminiani, who after 1714 passed the greater part of his life in England and Ireland. Through his sonatas and his concerti grossi, Opera II, III, and VII, he disseminated the forms in which his master had excelled. He transcribed into concertos Corelli's Opus V. Finally and above all, he founded an instructional method which transfused into England the experience of the Italian school.

Among Geminiani's pupils to win fame were Matthew Dubourg, a Corellian devotee from the very first, of whom it was claimed that he made his debut in 1712 at the age of nine playing a solo from Opus V while perched on a chair at Britton's concerts; the aesthetician, Avison, who in his writings would swear only by Corelli; the virtuosi John Clegg and Michael Festing, the latter a composer of sonatas and concertos in which the memory of Opus VI is evoked in some passages, flanked by others inspired by Albinoni and Vivaldi.

Pietro Castrucci, arriving a year after Geminiani in 1715, and Stefano Carbonelli, both of whom made their first appearances in London in 1720, were not, for all that their careers were less smooth and productive than Geminiani's, negligible elements in the campaign which culminated in the quasi-beatification of their master. In this campaign the London publishers, for their part, worked hard: after Walsh came Richard Meares, Benjamin Cooke, Daniel Wright, Johnson, Bremner, Preston, Cocks, and others besides, whose names will be found in the Musical Bibliography (see page 206). From 1731 to 1740 or thereabouts, an old employee of Walsh, William Smith, had a shop on the Strand with a sign board saying "Corelli's Head.'

The ascendancy of Handel and the later advent of Haydn, Mozart, and Beethoven were by and by to extinguish this zeal, yet without diminution of the respect which Corelli's name and work inspired. Shortly before the middle of the century the younger Nicola Matteis still played, as a normal thing, the sonatas of Opus V. Very much later, about 1790, Billington brought out through the firm of G. Walker the concertos of Opus VI, adapted for organ, harpsichord, or pianoforte, "as they are performed by Mr. Cramer." François Hippolyte Barthélémon, a native of Bordeaux who had settled in London, and a very great master now in unjust oblivion, at the concert of the *New Musical Fund* on the 24th of February, 1791, included a solo by Corelli; [119] he and his friend Johann Peter Salomon, a Rhinelander who had also made England his adopted home, were the very last followers. With their passing—Barthélémon in 1808, Salomon in 1815—admiration for Corelli was relegated into the archeological field.

In 1832 he even had a detractor, William Gardiner, who wrote in *The Music of Nature:* "For many years the lugubrious strains of Corelli were the only instrumental pieces performed in our theatres and they were described, at that time, as mirth-provoking music before the play." But William Bingley, two years later (*Musical Biography*, London, 1834, I, 287–291) showed unqualified enthusiasm based on an incontestable knowledge of Corelli's work. John Hullah, in his *History of Modern Music* of 1862, went further in his eulogy than any eighteenth-century panegyrist: "The progress of art," he wrote (p. 145), "is not always made on an inclined plane. It is checked from time to time by barriers which present no outlet, and are, to the common eye, inaccessible. Some of the most forbidding of these would seem to have been surmounted by the genius of Corelli. If there ever was an inventor, he was one. He would seem to have had no models—not even a point of departure; he did not improve, or correct, or mould, or transform; he created—the first music, pure and simple; and showed, first, that sounds have a connexion and a meaning of their own which, if less obvious and less precise than those of words, are no less intimate and profound."

It was in France that the influence of Corelli had the most unexpected results. It not only entailed the growth of a school of composer-performers very soon capable of vying with their model; but it also enhanced the status of the violin, which hitherto had been rejected as plebian by good society; while anticipating the Quarrel of the Bouffons, a furious altercation broke out at that time between the advocates of the French style and of the Italian.

Although violinists like Bocan and Constantin had known fashionable approval in a sporadic way, and others grouped in "bandes" had made themselves indispensable to the ballets, their instrument had never been able to gain admittance to the French salons on an equal footing with the lute, harpsichord, and bass viol. By reason of its more incisive sonority and its lowly beginnings in the hands of strolling players, the violin was left to lackies; and the repertoire of "pieces," such as those played on the viols and harpsichord, was proscribed for it. This magnificent instrumental soprano had to be content with playing for dances or in the tutti passages of operas.

To change that state of affairs required the double impact of a name that was supremely invested with renown and came from beyond the frontier, and of a musical form that was still novel in France despite the prestige it had enjoyed beyond the Alps for almost a century: *Corelli* and the *Sonata*.

A year after the success at Paris of the *Xerxes* of Cavalli, the death of Mazarin in 1661 was the signal for a violent reaction against the Italian music which the cardinal had been wont to patronize. *L'Ercole Amante*, so long awaited and so prematurely lauded, met only indifference in 1662. Henry Prunières, who has traced the history of these veerings in so masterly a way, shows that Lully assumed the lead of the cabal which aimed at making a clean sweep of his former compatriots and tolerating Italian music only in church where it could not overshadow his own.[120]

For all that, certain dilettanti were turning aside from Baptiste's operas and ballets and were impatiently waiting to become acquainted at last with these new Italian composers— Buononcini, Scarlatti, and Corelli—about whom travelers back from Rome and Venice gave them glowing accounts.

It was on the ecclesiastical flank that the counteroffensive was slowly mounted. A little later, at the height of the mêlée, one of the characters of the polemist Lecerf de la Viéville exclaimed: "I will name as many of them as you wish, not only musicians by profession, but people of quality, nay Prelates, who have given up singing and only have Italian pieces and sonatas played at their gatherings" (*Comparison*, II, 54). In fact, we know from Séré de Rieux and several others that the first and foremost introducer into France of these transalpine pieces was an Abbé Mathieu, curé of Saint-André-des-Arcs. Each week there was a concert at his home at which "these excellent works" filled the program.[121] The *Mercure Galant* of 1680 mentions concerts, similarly arranged, which were given at Dijon at the residence of M. de Malteste.

Matters were to reach the point where snobbery stepped in, even though the modern usage of the word was not yet current. Corelli's name began to be separated from that of Buononcini and the others, and, for an entire coterie, he symbolized the perfection of "contemporary" art.

One of the best proofs of this is the way in which the first French sonatas, which were composed by François Couperin in 1692, were brought out. Couperin belatedly published them in 1726 under the title of *Les Nations*, prefacing them with a "Composer's Confession to the Public." Here is a short excerpt:

The first Sonata of this Set was also the first that I composed, and the first to be composed in France. The actual history of it is singular. Delighted with those of Signor Corelli, whose works I shall love as long as I live, also with the French Works of Monsieur de Lully, I made so bold as to compose one similar, which I had performed at the Concert, where I heard those of Corelli; knowing the avidity of the French for foreign Novelties above all things, and, having no self-confidence, I did myself a very good service by a trifling official untruth. I pretended that a relative of mine, with the King of Sardinia, had sent me a Sonata by a new Italian

Composer: I arranged the letters of my name in such a way that they formed an Italian name which I used instead. The Sonata was devoured with eagerness; and I said nothing about an apology for it. What happened, however, encouraged me, and I wrote other sonatas; and my Italianate name, as a mask, earned me great commendations. My Sonatas, happily, won favor enough so that the deception did not make me blush.

Couperin's admiration for Corelli was not to wane. In his work he bore witness to it several times. André Pirro points out (*Les Clavecinistes*, p. 89) that *La Milordine* has the same outline as a gigue in Opus IV, and he mentions other points of similarity. But Couperin pays an even more explicit homage to Corelli in the *Grande sonade en Trio intitulée le Parnasse ou l'Apothéose de Corelli*, composed in 1722 or 1723 at the zenith of his career and published in 1724 in the collection *Les Goûts Réunis*. There, in a style in which allusions are frequent to the idiom of Corelli—not that Couperin's piquancy and harmonic inventiveness can be forgotten for a moment—we see seven short episodes successively represented: "Corelli au pied du Parnasse prie les Muses de le recevoir parmi elles" (Gravement, C); "Corelli, charmé de la bonne réception qu'on lui fait au Parnasse, en marque sa Joye. Il continue avec ceux qui l'accompagnent" (Gayment, 6/8); "Corelli buvant à la source d'Hypocrêne, Sa Troupe continüe" (2/2); "Entouziasme de Corelli causé par les eaux d'Hypocrêne" (Vivement, 3); "Corelli après son Entouziasme s'endort, et sa Troupe joue le Sommeil suivant très doux" (C); "Les Muses réveillent Corelli et le placent auprès d'Apollon" (Vivement, 3); "Remerciement de Corelli" (Gayment, C). Professor Manfred Bukofzer very rightly states (*op. cit.*, p. 249) that certain movements, in particular the first and the last, could easily be taken for authentic Corelli.

It did not need so much in this direction for Couperin to be accused of making himself "le serviteur passionné de l'Italien": the epithet was bestowed by Lecerf de la Viéville, of whom more anon, and Fausto Torrefranca is wrong to take it literally.[122] After a phase of youthful enthusiasm to which we owe the sonatas of 1692 and the subterfuge thanks to which they made their mark, Couperin built up a vocabulary and musical syntax which were entirely original. His *Apothéose de Corelli* was both act of deference to the memory of a great man and at the same time a gesture of diplomatic courtesy: a great French instrumental school had come into being which could, without humiliation, proffer a hand to Italian composers.

The point of view is defined with all desirable clarity in *L'Apothéose de Lully* of 1724, published in 1725. Couperin this time introduces the Florentine, to whom the Gods offer a place on Parnassus. Lully accepts at the invitation of Apollo. After the "welcoming between them and the greeting paid to Lully by Corelli and the Italian Muses," Lully thanks Apollo, who then exhorts the two leaders to unite their styles, a fusion of which must produce "the perfection of music." Whereupon they play together an *Essai en forme d'Ouverture*, then each an air in his own style; then the ensemble plays a short sonata entitled *La Paix du Parnasse*. Concerning this sonata, Professor Manfred Bukofzer writes: "Except for his church music Couperin has not written anything that can compare with the dignified and carefully wrought counterpoint of this sonata which seems to belie the thin texture of the rococo style" (*op. cit.*, p. 249).

There is reason to believe that the idea of this rapprochement was in the air. The year (1725) of the *Apothéose de Lully*, an "Idyll in music by Monsieur Bouret" (Bouret wrote only the words, the composer not being named) called *Le Triomphe des Mélophilètes* appeared, using the same allegorical plot. The work has not been preserved, but from the account of it given in the *Mercure de France* (December, 1725), we know that in the fifth scene "a chorus was sung, followed by a short prelude for Mercury, who goes on to give account to Apollo of the commission which he had given him to evoke the shades of Lully and of Corelli." The "Illustrious Shades" appear and Apollo addresses them with a heartfelt apostrophe. Music by both in turn, performed by the Mélophilètes, whereupon the shade of Corelli concludes:

> Ils ont embelli leur modèle
> En prêtant à nos airs une grâce nouvelle.
> C'est nous rendre encor plus qu'ils n'ont reçu de nous;
> Mais bien loin d'en être jaloux
> Nous rentrons satisfaits dans la nuit éternelle.*

Such is the similarity of subject matter and concordance of dates that there would be no great risk in conjecturing some connection; either that in the "Idyll" Bouret had reworked

---

* They have embellished their model
By lending to our airs a grace that's novel.
In this repaying yet more than they received from us
But far indeed from being jealous
Contented we shall return into eternal night.

and expanded the Concert of Couperin, or that the composer, having set to music the *Triomphe des Mélophilètes*, retained only the purely instrumental parts of it for publication and from them formed the *Apothéose de Lully*.

But we must now turn to the musical events which occurred in the meantime. Dating from the year 1695, that is, three years after Couperin's innocent subterfuge, are sonatas by Jean-Fery Rebel, Sébastien de Brossard, and Elisabeth-Claude Jacquet de Laguerre; and these latter no longer embarrassed themselves with pseudonyms. The extraordinary sensation of Corelli's Opus V further stimulated "this passion for composing sonatas in the Italian manner," which had invaded French music. "What joy, what a fine opinion of himself has a man who knows something of the fifth Opera of Corelli!" sneered Lecerf de la Viéville.

Between 1700 and 1723, the year in which Leclair's first book was published—the veritable leader of the French school, the "Corelly of France" as Blainville said later—more than thirty sets of sonatas appeared; some were by foreigners—Italians such as Mascitti, Piani, Fedeli, and Englishmen such as Henry Eccles; yet the great majority were by French composers, of whom several were decidedly no mere imitators. Lionel de la Laurencie has shed the most revealing light on the first efforts of sonata composers in France, on the ties which linked them with their prototypes, and on the worth of their personal contributions which was considerable as far as Duval, Senaillé, Francoeur the younger and Jean-Fery Rebel were concerned. I can only refer the reader to the classic work on the subject, *L'Ecole française de violon*.

It must not be thought that in France Corelli's influence

was limited to the sonata: fine Corellian touches have been pointed out recently in the cantatas of Bernier [123] (about 1703); Dandrieu interpolated "La Corelli" among the pieces of his *Deuxième livre pour le clavecin* (1727); Blavet transcribed the gavottes of Opus V for the flute; Spourni published under the initials V. S. some *Sonate a tre, Due Violini e Basso. Imitatione del Signor Corelli;* innumerable "Folies d'Espagne" for violin, guitar, mandolin, flute, and harp kept up the memory of the *follia* until the end of the century; theorists borrowed examples from Corelli's adagios or dances.[124]

Publishers in France decided to engrave Opus V later than did English publishers; Foucault about 1701, Charlotte Massard de la Tour in 1708, and then Ballard. The other works followed. There was not a library of an amateur or institution in the eighteenth century which did not possess almost the entire corpus of Corelli's work.[125] The Academy of Lyons made room for him even during the early days from 1713 to 1718 when few Italian works were played.[126] At the inaugural performance of the *Concerts Spirituels*, on March 18, 1725, a conspicuous place in the very middle of the programme was allotted to the Christmas Eve concerto: the work remained in the repertoire of this venerable institution until 1766.

Moreover, the violin, thanks to the pre-eminence over other instruments which the sonata conferred on it, penetrated by degrees among "people of worth." Lecerf de la Viéville wrote in 1705: "In France this instrument is not a noble one . . . but a man of rank who takes a fancy to playing the violin does not demean himself." In 1738 the *Mercure de France* was obliged to admonish noblemen who made public display of

their talent as violinists and vied with professionals. The "enthusiasm" engendered in the earliest years of the century must
have been powerful, and the reign of the sonata inexorable,
for such a musico-social upheaval to have come about.

Still, resistance elements were not lacking. The champions
of the keyboard and of the viol, and composers of the old
school were more or less openly up in arms. Marais did not
cease "to inveigh against sonatas." [127] Saint-Lambert in his
Nouveau traité de l'accompagnement (1707) discreetly observed that there were some people who allowed "bad progressions" in accompaniments; and that "such were to be found
in the Sonnantes [*sic*] of the famous Corelli, now so celebrated
in Europe, and fashionable with us for some years past."

But above all, a widespread campaign of criticism—a new
situation in France—was staged, which furnished not just
articles and lampoons, but actual volumes in the war of French
aestheticians.

The quarrel which was foolishly incited in 1702 by the
*Parallele des Italiens et des François en ce qui regarde la
musique et les opéra,* wherein the Abbé Raguenet, with no-
torious maladroitness, lauded the merits of France's rivals, has
been sketched and commented upon already. I will only
pause over the crux of the matter, the reply in some seven
hundred closely printed duodecimo pages which Lecerf de la
Viéville de Freneuse, a Minister of Justice in the Parliament of
Rouen, made to him. His *Comparaison de la musique italienne
et de la musique françoise,*[128] several passages from which I
have cited earlier, defines in an ingenious and spirited way a
French aesthetic of clarity, simplicity, and reason which is
easily reconciled with what we know of the spirit of the *grand*

siècle. In detail it defends the opera of Lully against the lyrical Italian school, especially represented in the person of Buononcini, and defends French instrumental music against that of Corelli. With regard to Corelli, la Viéville reacted with a violence and injustice which are surprising. He reproached Corelli with outraging good taste by the incoherence of his style, the extravagance of his passage work, the monotony of his repetitions, and above all "the acerbity of his dissonances."

At the beginning of the polemic he imputed to Corelli 14 consecutive fourths "in a piece which I can't recall," and 26 sixths in the 11th sonata of Opus IV. The Abbé Raguenet took advantage of this vagueness to cast doubts on the competence of la Viéville, and the latter replied with a sweeping charge against the harmony of Corelli:

I think that he [the Abbé Raguenet] will find them [the sixths] in the Prélude of this 11th sonata: three at first and twenty-three in serried mass afterward, in two different parts. And in order to try and give him a less sorry opinion of me, I draw his attention to the fact that in this Prélude alone, which has only twenty-four measures, he will find over and over again all the faulty progressions imaginable, without any "supposition" to assuage them. [This is a matter of melodic movement, the progression of voices; "supposition" in this context means a passing note.] A skip of a diminished fourth without an intervening third in the second treble voice of the first measure, a skip of a diminished fifth in the bass voice of the second measure, a tritone in the same measure, a skip of a major sixth in the second treble voice of the fourth measure, a skip of a ninth in the second treble voice of the ninth measure, and goodness knows what else? These progressions, as the Abbé well knows, are contrary to all the rules. They seem placed here in spite of the rules, in order to make sport of them and of the coherence and sweetness of the melodies, and they create insufferable effects into the bargain. He will discover also a veritable funeral toll in the seventeenth, eighteenth, nineteenth, and twentieth measures, useless repetitions everywhere; and, what is worse to my thinking, the uppermost voice is always utterly poverty-stricken with only a vestige of melody; finally, he will find twelve consecutive sevenths in a measure and a half, and this twice over, etc. (*Comparaison*, IV, 202)

Need it be said that these strictures are flagrantly exaggerated, that the progressions so acrimoniously pointed out exhibit no offensive feature, and that the consecutive sixths and sevenths are of different species, which renders their sequence perfectly legitimate?

But our critic is angry, nor does he conceal his chagrin: "I ask pardon for this from French Musicians. Up to now I have flattered this Corelli. The fear of appearing partial and prejudiced has led me into too many reservations. When Monsieur the Abbé asks me, I will really criticize the 11th Sonata. . . ." (II, 203). So as not to prolong this chapter unduly, I will not discuss all of la Viéville's points, directed as much against the composer of the sonatas as against the violinists, organists, and harpsichordists who swore only by Corelli.

The pity of it is that la Viéville's book, whatever verve he expended in it, remains beside the point. The "balanced" part of it, so to speak, the appraisal of the merits of Lully and of his school, is perfectly cogent. But the extravagance of the reproaches leveled at the Italians, and against Corelli in particular, deprives him of all convincing force—especially for us, for whom the passage of time often blurs dissimilarities between two sides, although two centuries earlier such dissimilarities may likely have provoked strife.

Let us not be too quick to tax ourselves with myopia. A leveling process of this sort happens faster than one may think. The author of the *Lettres sur la musique Françoise en réponse à celle de J. J. Rousseau* (1754) accused the Italians of his generation of having forgotten the old simplicity in order "to shine, to flit about, and to caper"; in his opinion, "at the time of Lully and of Corelli, the two musicks, Italian and French, were almost the same." For Hawkins, Lully and Corelli together "are to be looked on as the first great improvers of that kind of instrumental harmony which for a full half century has been practised and admired throughout Europe" (II, 754). From the Italian side, Arteaga extolled Corelli for "his adroitness at reconciling the taste of the two nations." [129] In point of fact, an objective study of Corelli's music has shown us that he bore no aversion toward French dance forms or the Lullian overtures.

Moreover, Lecerf de la Viéville and those whose self-appointed spokesman he was achieved nothing for their pains. The response of composers in the domain of practical music has already been seen: I allude to the sets of French sonatas before which the *pièces* steadily lost ground. Only harpsichordists and violists continued to write these, and yet in so doing they incorporated contours, "batteries," broken chord figures, and even structural features borrowed from the idiom of the Italian violinists.

As occurs often enough, the theorists yielded in their turn. After 1715–1720 French theorists are pro-Corellian to a man.

From the innumerable professions of faith we will select that
of Séré de Rieux, whose doggerel verses have a certain savor.
In his epistle *La Musique* he first of all introduces the reactionary *mélomane*:

> Loin de nous les auteurs dont la fière Italie
> Etale vainement la sçavante folie.
> Chez eux tout est extrême, et jamais de bon sens
> Ne régla leurs desseins ou trop vifs, ou trop lents.
> Leur sonate à Lully n'eût paru qu'un caprice
> Propre à former la main par un vif exercice. . . .*

To which the author replies, through the lips of the informed
amateur:

> Mais par le temps au vrai le sage accoûtumé
> De sa prévention cesse enfin d'être armé
> Et d'un goût étranger l'exacte connoissance
> Détruit les préjugés qu'inspire la naissance.
> De la Sonate ainsi reconnoissant le prix,
> Par un docte progrès en France on fut épris.
> Déjà par ce chemin la sçavante Italie
> A versé sur nos sens une aimable folie.
> Corelli par ses sons enleva tous les coeurs. . . .† [130]

*   From us avaunt, musicians in whom proud Italy
     Displays in vain her artful folly.
     In whom all is extreme, and n'er good sense
     Did rule their forms, too fast or slow, and hence
     Their sonata à Lully seemed but caprice—wise,
     Suited to train the hand, by lively exercise.
†   But the wise man by time to truth accustomed,
     At last with bias ceases to be armed,
     And the just knowledge of a foreign style
     Ends preconceptions, birth-inspired erstwhile.
     Thus the Sonata's worth we recognizing,
     Its sage advance in France were idolizing.
     Already by this way has artful Italy,
     Over our senses poured a lovely folly.
     Corelli by his tones enraptured every heart.

The fatuous Hubert Le Blanc, waging party warfare against the violin in order to defend too late the interests of the violists, makes obeisance before a name which is no longer disputed: "Continuing one's way, one feels halted, and powerless to progress beyond Corelli. *Quo me fessum rapis, Corelli, tu maximus ille es.* It is a moot point whether this Inventor of the sonata may not have seized upon, once and for all, the good in Instrumental Music; and like Homer, finding no one in the past to serve as his model, he no more would find anyone in the future imitating." [131]

And here, for the opposite faction, is the Abbé Pelegrin: [132] "Corelli began to give his works to the public in 1700: today there is still to be found in them beauty of melody, beauty of character, cadences in the French style, a beautiful fluidity; such "batteries" as there may be are moderated and adroitly placed; it is an elegant music which lovers of the recherché find too simple today, as is the case with Lully's operas. The Italians of our time vehemently turn away from it."

It is a unanimous concert of acclamations and eulogies. The final quibble consisted of claiming Corelli as a pure product of Lully's teaching: "It is an established fact that Corelli acknowledged that he owed his music to Lully, that great master of Music in France [!]. So then, it is we who have fashioned Italian music" (Travenol, *La Galerie de l'Académie Royale de musique*, 1754, p. 33).

IV

Conclusion

AS I pointed out at the beginning of this book, and as the reader may have gathered during his reading, my hero no longer appears in quite the same light as in the first study I devoted to him. Good faith demands my confessing to this and briefly indicating the motives behind my change of attitude.

In the first place, the tone of hagiography which prevailed with a good many of Corelli's biographers had impelled me, by way of reaction, to take the side of the "objective" historians of the school of Riehl, Andreas Moser, and Ecorcheville: with enhanced perspective, their objectivity seems to me scarcely less tendentious than the lyrical excesses against which I had sought to be on my guard.

Secondly, a longstanding familiarity with Vivaldi, and one more recent with Albinoni and Bonporti led me to prefer the coruscant and imaginative quality of their invention to the sagacity of the creation of Corelli.

Finally, although I had a thorough knowledge of the sonatas for violin and bass of Opus V, a knowledge, I might add, based on audition and on perusal, the rest of the work (apart from the Christmas Eve concerto) was only familiar to me through reading the scores. But the instrumental music written in the period of 1650–1750, and more particularly that of the Italians, can only be properly judged by hearing it, by virtue of a characteristic which has not been stressed as much it should be; namely that composers of this school, performers all of them, had a sense of sonority which made them use, probably instinctively, the richest blendings not only of the upper harmonies but also of low-pitched tones suitable for giving body to the bass parts. So that pieces for strings, whose texture in two or three voices may seem thin and schematized when merely reading the score, have, for the ear, an amazing completeness. The recent revival of the chamber orchestra continues to offer confirmation of this fact. Corelli is one of the chief beneficiaries of the revival, for the new ensembles have enlarged their repertoire hitherto based on Bach and Vivaldi. The tercentenary of the birth of the master of Fusignano marked him as among the first due for their attention; and the listener was soon persuaded that he stood the comparison and that his concertos—with their quite diverse characteristics, more sombre eloquence, and more archaic structure— ranked with the Brandenburgs and *L'Estro Armonico*.

This is not to say that the most immoderate panegyrists must be blindly followed.

Starting with the Quarrel of the Bouffons, the Corellian factionists were no longer in accord as to their reasons for praising Corelli.[133] Some made him out as a man of sensibility, others a man of speculation; he was all instinct or all reason, as the case required. Whether the violinist or the composer in him was exalted, he was invariably conceded first place, at least chronologically, as though he had retrieved the violin and indeed all instrumental music from chaos. It was J. B.

Cartier, a writer most devoted to historical truth, who nevertheless wrote: "Before Corelli the art of violin playing was absolutely unknown: the employment of this instrument was left to the rule of thumb practice of some ignorant musicians who could not be qualified by the honourable title of artists." [134] To which, without inhibition, Paul Stoeving added an echo: "It was Corelli who raised fiddling to the dignity of an art, by the side of the other reproductive arts; who first (in his own land at least) freed it from mediaeval tavern and trampdom reminiscences, and the fiddler from the unsavoury reputation of quackery and trickery and smelling of strong drinks which hitherto had clung round him like wet clothes round a swimmer. . . ." [135]

In the matter of composition, Choron, a scholar of balanced outlook, attributed to Corelli before Maroncelli's doing so the same outstanding merit as an inventor: "Corelli who was alive in 1700 was the first to wean instrumental music from its infant state. . . . The sonatas of Corelli aroused general emulation: soon performers and composers appeared, not only for the violin, but even for (and moreover on Corelli's model) the other instruments. Three ages may be distinguished in the progress of instrumental music; the first commencing with Corelli. . . ." [136] And this leads, after three or four generations of commentators, to the following effusion, the pleasure of quoting which I cannot resist: "It was some enterprise to have the sarabandes of Arcangelo Corelli performed on the little violins of Médard with their gaudy varnish and indifferent tone; these sarabandes warm with passion, of amorous murmurs, and of flowers gilded by the southern sun, palpitating, deeply moved, and tragic as a poem of Ariosto. This was music for Watteau, for whom Italy would ever be unattained; a little of the harmonies he would have found there, of the bright day, of the beautiful valiance of sunlit outlines, a little of the proud wantoness of the women of Naples and of Venice. . . ." [137]

Now what have we found of all this in investigating the music itself and the art of the violinist?

I know that one must needs show extreme prudence in trying to appreciate the idioms of past epochs, fashioned as they were for sensibilities differing from ours. I know that a single chord to which our ear has become blasé could provoke uproars, that a passage which today is stale might then overwhelm a listener by its unexpectedness. Having said this, it yet remains nevertheless impossible to accept Corelli as an innovator in a revolutionary sense. Riehl has said so emphatically, and so has Moser, both of them experienced historians who knew and admired their man. Ecorcheville goes even further: [138] "The foundation of Corelli's character is the absence and mistrust of audacious novelties. This temperament was partly the reason for his fame. His originality lay in not having any. It is because he halted and remained in the domain conquered before him without seeking new horizons, it is because he exploited on the spot, so to speak, those riches that had been accumulated for over a century, that Corelli has left a work *perenius aere*." Without going so far as this denial of all personality—for it requires character to maintain one's conservatism with this composure and stolidity—we recognize that this verdict of Ecorcheville contains a certain element of truth beneath its exaggeration. The violin technique in the most daring passages of Opus V pales beside that of a Uccellini, and even more beside that of a Walther or a Biber. D'Angeli has shown how much from the point of view of form had been achieved before Corelli by Pesanti and by Fontana; [139] and Vatielli has reconstructed the contribution of the old Bolognese School, while stressing that which separates the Bolognese precursors from their disciple in his eventual status as a master: "He has brought this style [the Bolognese] to a crystalline purity, he has raised it to a point of classic perfection, and truly the pinion of his genius soars into regions of sublime beauty which the older Bolognese could not hope to attain with all their talents. Moreover, they were the first to acknowledge his great merit and admire the work of one whom they called 'the new Orpheus of our time.' " [140]

Here we touch upon the message, the very heart of Corelli's music. A historian who is also an artist, Fausto Torrefranca, sees in it "pathetic strains, a sonorous plenitude that, vibrant and sustained, hints to us of an intimate and communicative sensuality. But this music is yet more often suffused with a *raptus* of almost ascetic spirituality, especially in the slow movements." [141] The same commentator sees in the fugal *allegros* of the church sonatas in Opus V "a miracle of exquisite polyphony for solo violin."

I confess myself unable to follow Torrefranca on this last issue: these fugues with their short and arid themes soon become brittle, whereas the fugues of the trio sonatas, less constrained by difficulties of instrumental technique, enhance the beauty of a contrapuntal texture. Professor Bukofzer has shown the extent to which this contributed to the elaboration of modern harmony.

The pathetic strains are relatively rare, nor was it by them that Corelli conquered his audience. Rather, his musicality was distinguished, as I have been at pains to show in this book, by a suavity, a never overpowering nobility, a restrained wistfulness save for one or two poignant *adagios*, a simple and healthy gaiety, and, above all, by an extraordinary flair for blending sonorities, apparent more than anywhere else in the concerti grossi.

Does one really feel in the presence of a genius? Is there a common element between Corelli and that whirlwind of music, Vivaldi, perpetually pouring forth melodies, rhythms, harmonies, still as alive, for the most part, as on the day of their creation?

Here is a profound problem. Corelli had experienced in his day the consecration of a fame which on his death merely increased. Vivaldi knew fitful flares of renown, followed by complete neglect. His death passed unnoticed: for him no tomb at the Rotunda, no national homage. The date of his death has but recently been discovered, as well as the town where he was so meanly buried that there is no trace of his grave. Such is but a normal turn of events. The astounding thing is the success of Corelli, rapid and conclusive, such as neither Bach nor Mozart knew.

The reason for this is not to be found solely in his talent as a performer, exceptional as this conceivably may have been. The crowd, even that of the salons, does not react spontaneously to an art form so stripped of the seductions of virtuosity. Reputations based on style are generally the longest in getting established.

Corelli's character and culture were bound to help to a great degree here. The majority of his rivals, unstable, itinerant, led worldly lives with a proverbial insouciance. By contrast we see Corelli calm, reflective, cultured, contemplating his art with a religious respect, and having no other passion, at least as far as we know, than painting or music. He is settled; people go to him because his personality possesses a certain radiance. Such is his ascendancy that the social barriers relegating musicians to a sort of domestic role, more or less acceptable, give way before him. No doubt that thanks to him the profession benefitted by a respect which was something quite new.

Another factor in his success was the coherence and continuity of his effort. He alone had sufficient self-restraint to write without haste, to deliver to the public at intervals of many years works which followed one another like chapters of a book which had taken a long time to polish, and to deny himself any incursion into a domain other than the one where he knew he was a master.

The environment in which the patronage of Cardinal Ottoboni placed him perhaps played the most important role in the build up of this fame. We have seen that snobbery made Corelli *de rigeur* in France. This was but an extension of his Roman vogue.

Talent, character, and circumstance placed him in the front rank. Then occurred one of those phenomena of crystalization of which each generation provides us with one or two examples. Our need for unanimity is a strange thing. An era cannot have two idols at the same time. When opposing waves sweep into one another, the first to reach a crest drains up all. A deeper and deeper gulf yawned between Corelli and his rivals whose prospects were hardly less than his. A single name figures in conversations and reports, and this notoriety gathers like a gigantic snowball. The ill-informed play their part; how many people have bandied in smart conversation the names of Wagner, Debussy, Stravinsky, Honegger, before having heard a single note written by them? Certainly the Abbé Raguenet showed himself up as a fool when he accused Lecerf de la Viéville, a knowledgeable musician, of taking Corelli for an operatic composer by virtue of the *Cinquième Opéra*.[142] But this is the type of snobbish blunder which many others could have made and which, by accretion, had appreciable results. Gossip, polemics, travelers' tales—all this accretes over the just praises of the outset to end, in the course of time, in the "chaste and faultless Corelli" of Avison, in an admiration based on trust, in a sort of *élan mystique*.

This is to be regretted for the injustice thus done to those whom such brilliance has relegated to obscurity with the collusion of our own laziness. The excellent biographer of Bassani, Francesco Pasini, has protested against this in vigorous terms: "A great fuss," he says, "is worked up about certain names and certain works: at all costs it is sought to epitomize a long series of efforts and all the labor of a long era of artists in these few names and in these few works—the peaks, so we are told, of an ascending range. Despite all that is said and done, it is labor in vain; the arbitrary element strikes us too forcibly, and the feeling of our own ignorance becomes more distressing as we dimly perceive the extreme importance of this period."[143]

This is obviousness itself, and it would be intolerable if the justified honors bestowed on Corelli entailed, as a corollary, the forgetting of a whole world of composers who were industrious, inspired, and sometimes geniuses, and who quarried the materials that he used.

Corelli's greatest claim to the gratitude and admiration of musicians lies not so much in his novelty or creative power as in the opportuneness of his appearance and the steadfastness of his influence just at the time when there was needed a leader of a "School" around whom to rally. Riehl has shown us that Corelli was the link between two musical epochs—between the counterpoint of the seventeenth century and the melodic emancipation of the eighteenth. In this respect, however, his position was no different from that of Bassani, Torelli, and Buononcini. Angelo Berardi, in his *Miscellanea Musicale* of 1689, takes pride in having composed many works, "always new and varied and corresponding to the two styles, the old and the new." In these years more than one composer had a clear conception of being in a transitional period. But Corelli understood it better than any other, took his bearings, and from thence regulated his course. His path from the old polyphony to harmonic texture is a marvel of sagacity. Just as he knew how to reconcile the almost conflicting tendencies of Bologna and of Rome, "the first more learned, the second more idealist," according to d'Angeli, so he evolved without any stress between the past and the future as he saw it. And throughout his career he never ceased to affirm the tonality principle by which classical, romantic, and most contemporary musicians were to live.

Critics of great discernment, such as Riehl, admire Corelli first and foremost as a composer, deploring that in the eyes of his contemporaries he had been concealed by the virtuoso. They see his trios, rather than the numerous Italian trios of the first half of the eighteenth century, as the true precursors of the classical quartet; and in his concertos the key to the orchestra of Bach.

As for the origins of the quartet, matters are less simple; elements other than the preclassical trio come into play, beginning with the fantasias and consorts for viols in which England of the seventeenth century was so rich. Then again, although Corelli has a front rank in the domain of the trio, he was heavily indebted to forerunners, starting with Cazzati, who had prepared the paths for him.

As to the concerti grossi, I have tried earlier to pay to their wonderful success the respect which is their due. Yet, while fully recognizing their superiority, and perhaps even that of Opus III, over the sonatas of Opus V, it is right to attribute to Opus V and to Corelli, the violinist, a supreme importance in the destiny of music. That quality which confers the prize on the sonatas—considering them for their intrinsic worth— namely, the restraint in expression which modern sensibility may deprecate in them, served as a positive factor and a truly efficacious leaven at the time they appeared. In the eyes of Corelli's followers, a master of his standing would not have adhered to so discreet a style of composition without due reason. Gifted for the violin to the degree that has been reported, he was clearly able to venture difficult techniques as well as his predecessors, or better, and to explore quite new regions of acrobatic virtuosity, even if he showed himself less strict as to purity of style. He, whose bow possessed so much persuasive charm, could have sought, too, the response which cheap pathos invariably raises.

His abstention in this had didactic value, and in itself demanded great force of character. This renunciation, this "stripping down," of Opus V has only the appearance of timidity. For, on the contrary, it betokened a striving toward clarity, sobriety, and good taste against a possible encroachment of the baroque and of originality at any price; an analogous reaction to that which, as Andrea d'Angeli has shown, Salvator Rosa, Redi, and Tassoni led in literature against Preti, Achillini, and Marini.

Perhaps I have put too much stress on this exclusively moral point of view, and thus incurred the risk of abasing the work to favor its composer; if this is true, I am the victim of my own expository ineptitude.

Attempting, in conclusion, to sum up my position as lucidly as possible—with due reservations in respect to new facts relevant to an appreciation which cannot be based entirely on concrete evidence—the epithet of "genius" traditionally associated with Corelli's name undoubtedly has not quite the same connotation as when ascribed to a Vivaldi or a Bach. It does not imply the same high soaring; but instead a constant perfection, a voluntary moderation, and an exemplary sense of proportion.

If, relatively speaking, he innovated little, if it is unfair to concentrate in his person the result of a century of evolution during which the primitive sonata was fashioned, we are indebted to him for its most harmonious examples in the forms which he worked out. His style exists, suave and ample; there is a Corellian melody, harmony, and counterpoint. Formative elements were to be found in his forerunners of Bologna and of Rome; no one else gave them a similar seal of achievement, so much plenitude, order, simplicity.

Those very works which are most dated are models of balanced euphony and most beautiful historical prototypes. And several trio sonatas, almost all of Opus V, and all the concertos could resume their place in the repertoire.

Corelli's influence rests unimpaired, and has a cogency which can never be sufficiently stressed. The religion of his art inspired this placid man with the energy to institute himself as the champion of an order which was necessary in a generally deteriorating Italy. Moral indiscipline was facilitating every folly, and this was the time when throughout Europe musicians were expecting a great transition. By preventing its premature development, by channeling into progressive reform, by all his authority, what might have turned into revolution and chaos, Corelli contributed greatly to the advent of classicism. In a positive way he established, as a virtuoso, a classicism of performance to which all violin schools have since referred. Had nothing of his written work lasted, we should still be his debtors.

V

Notes

1. This first chapter, particularly as far as the period of Corelli's youth is concerned, borrows extensively from the labors of Dr. Carlo Piancastelli (*In Onore di Arcangelo Corelli*), who has completely recast Corelli's biography. To his researches I owe all the details relative to the ancestors of the master of Fusignano and to the testimony of the Abbé Laurenti.

2. Crescimbeni calls her Santa Baruzzi (*Notizie*, 1720, I, 250).

3. *Cf.* Vatielli, *Il Corelli e i maestri bolognesi*, pp. 151, 161–64.

4. Vatielli, *op. cit.*, pp. 178–80. Rinaldi's objection that Corelli and Laurenti were both pupils of Benvenuti—he writes "together," but what do we know of this?—is worthless. G. B. Laurenti, born in 1644, was nine years older than Corelli; he had studied under Ercole Gaïbara and could have had something to teach the budding Corelli.

5. Ernst Ortlepp, *Grosses Instrumental- und Vokal-Concert*, Part 15, Stuttgart, 1841. This is only plagiarism of a stupid yarn of Stephen de la Madelaine, in "Corelli," *Revue et Gazette musicale de Paris*, November 13, 1836. But A. Pougin *Le Violon*, 1924, p. 81, has grounds for believing that Ortlepp's account appeared before this date in a periodical from which de la Madelaine took it.

6. I made this mistake despite the warning of Vidal in a monograph, now dated. "Les Violonistes," *Les Instruments à archet*, II (1877), 111.

7. A. Cametti, writing me from Rome on the 8th of March, 1932, corroborated that only Crescimbeni, who drafted his work in 1720, advanced this date of 1671; but no recorded evidence avouches for Corelli's presence in Rome before 1675.

8. *Lettre sur la Musique françoise*, 2nd ed., 1753, p. 45.

9. Mainwaring, *Memoirs of the Life of the late George Frederic Handel*, London, 1760, p. 46. *Cf.* also Hawkins, II, 674; Perotti, *Dissertation sur l'état actuel de la Musique en Italie*, trans. by C. B. Genoa, 1812, p. 7; Maroncelli, *Vita di Arcangiolo Corelli*, § VI; and Arteaga, *Le Rivoluzioni del Teatro musicale Italiano*, 2nd ed., Venice, 1785, II, 24.

10. Titon du Tillet, *La Parnasse françois*, Paris, 1732, p. 396.

11. Pierre de Morand, *Justification de la Musique françoise contra la querelle qui lui a été faite par un Allemand et un Allobroge*, La Haye, 1754, p. 52.

12. *Corelli*, pp. 46–55.

13. Note of Padre Martini reproduced by F. Vatielli, *op. cit.*, p. 161, following Alfredo Bonora who in 1913 gave it in the paper *Il Resto del Carlino*.

14. "Arcangelo Corelli à Saint-Louis-des-Français-à-Rome," *Revue Musicale*, January, 1922.

15. *Paralele* (*sic*) *des Italiens et des François en ce qui regarde la Musique et les Opéra*, Paris, 1702, p. 110.

16. W. K. Printz von Waldthurn, *Phrynidis Mytilenaei . . . dritter Theil*, Dresden, 1696, p. 227. "I travelled further on to Munich, where the famous violinist Herr Corelli had published several beautiful pieces. . . ."

17. Gerber, *Neues hist.-biogr. Lexikon*, 1812, I, col. 781, who simply duplicates Hawkins, II, 674. Pougin is more positive than all his predecessors, without the shadow of any new argument. *Cf. Le Violon*, Paris, 1924, p. 67.

18. Chrysander, *G. F. Händel,* 1898, I, 357*n.*

19. A. Einstein, "Italienische Musiker am Hofe der Neuburger Wittelsbacher," *Sammelbände der internationalen Musikgesellschaft,* IX, 414 ff.

20. Dr. Alfred Einstein undertook in respect to this subject protracted and fruitless researches among the archives at Munich. He willingly confirmed for me by letter the absence of any information, and expressed to me his very convincing hypothesis. In his *Musicalisches Lexikon* of 1732, J. G. Walther, on the authority of Printz alone, declared that "Corelli in 1680 was in the service of the Elector of Bavaria." It is this comment which Hawkins, Gerber, and others have enlarged upon.

21. Dr. Piancastelli dates these events from February (*op. cit.,* p. 43). The date of the arrival in Rome of the Earl of Castlemain must be advanced consequent on the *Ragguaglio della solemne comparsa fatta in Roma gli otto di Gennaio 1687, dall'ill. conte de Castelmaine . . . alla santa sede apostolica,* etc., Rome Ant. Ercole (1687). In this connection there is involved a concert given at the residence of Christina of Sweden with one hundred *musici* (singers) and 150 *suonatori* (instrumentalists). With respect to Christina of Sweden and the music, *cf.* De Bildt, *Christine de Suède et le cardinal Azzolino,* Paris, 1899, and especially A. Cametti, *Christina di Svezia, l'arte musicale e gli spettacoli teatrali in Roma,* Rome, 1931.

22. L. L. Valdrighi, "Cappelle, concerti e musiche di Casa d'Este," *Atti . . . di storia patria per le provincie Modenesi e Parmenesi,* Series III, Vol. II, Second Part, 486 and 492. Also see A. Moser, *Geschichte des Violinspiels,* Berlin, 1923, p. 70, who believes in the reality of this stay at Modena. He takes his stand on Corelli's Opus III having appeared in 1689 at Rome and Modena, dedicated to Francis II, Duke of Modena, and on the fact that the library of this latter town possesses many of the works of Corelli, either printed or in manuscript.

23. Edward J. Dent, *Alessandro Scarlatti*, London, 1905, p. 74. As early as 1702 Crescimbeni, in his *Comentari intorno alla sua istoria della volgar Poesia*, p. 148, spoke in glowing terms of these concerts given at the cardinal's, and "regolati da Arcagnolo (*sic*) Corelli, famoso professore di Violino." The influence of Ottoboni was already considerable. Numerous musicians had dedicated their works to him, among them Albinoni (Trio Sonatas, Opus IV, 1694), and Mascitti (Opus V, Paris, 1714). The *Osservazioni per ben regolare il Coro della Cappella Pontificia*, by Adami da Bolsena, Rome, 1711, contained an epistle addressed to him, as well as his portrait by F. Trevisani, engraved by L. Frey. In 1739 Charles de Brosses, who complained of having been received by Ottoboni with hierarchical coolness, limned a hardly flattering sketch of him: "He is old and decrepit, very discredited by his morals, having been a very gross man all his life, and not very circumspect regarding decorum on this account" (*Lettres familières*, published in Paris, 1885, II, 121); ". . . without manners, without credit, debauched, ruined, lover of the arts, a fine musician" (p. 347). "Ruined" must be understood as referring to his physique, as the obituary article devoted to Ottoboni by the *Gentleman's Magazine* of March, 1740—he died on the 17th of February—informs us that he held title to "nine abbeys in the Ecclesiastical State, five others in that of Venice, and three in France."

24. Pointed out by Piancastelli, *op. cit.*, p. 45. Only their libretto by Francesco Mario Paglia has been found. The title moreover runs: *Musica di Gio. Lorenzo Lulier* (undoubtedly the vocal music), *concerti d'Arcangelo Corelli* (undoubtedly the symphonic interludes, which may have been true concerti grossi).

25. Quoted by G. Hart, *The Violin and Its Music*, London, 1881, p. 183.

26. The *Catalogo dei maestri . . . della Congregazione ed Accademia di Santa Cecilia di Roma*, Rome, 1845, calls him, in 1700,

the "Guardiano della sez. strumentisti della Congregazione." F. Piovano, *Beiträge zu Rob. Eitner's Quellen Lexikon*, III, 17.

27. M. Rinaldi, *Arcangelo Corelli*, Milan, 1953.

28. C. F. Piancastelli, *op. cit.* Also receiving preferment were P. Antoni Fenaruoli da Brescia, D. Niccolo d'Aragona Napol. Principe di Cassano (Crescimbeni, *L'Arcadia*, Rome, 1711, p. 368).

29. J. B. Mancini, *Réflexions pratiques sur le chant figuré*, trans. by Rayneval, Paris, 1794, p. 16.

30. Burney, *History of Music*, III, 552–54. *Cf.* also Burgh, *Anecdotes of Music*, II, 260–63.

31. Dent, *op. cit.*, pp. 92–93. The manuscript of *Laodice* should read "Ti rendo amor," not "Ti rende ancor."

32. Rinaldi, *op. cit.*, pp. 249–50.

33. Benedetto, Croce, *I Teatri di Napoli*, 1891, p. 222. I am indebted to Andrea della Corte for this clue: "Corelli a Napoli," *Il Giornale*, April 1, 1953.

34. U. Prota Giurleo, "Breve Storia del Teatro di Corte," *Il Teatro di Corte del Palazzo Reale di Napoli*, a collection of studies published by F. de Filippis, Naples, 1952, p. 67.

35. Mistaken identity, according to Dr. Alfred Einstein, *op. cit.*, p. 414, between Corelli and Torelli: but Torelli was still alive and lived on until February 8, 1709.

36. Mainwaring, *op. cit.*, pp. 56–57.

37. According to A. Schering, "Zum Thema: Händel's Entlehnungen," *Sammelbände der internationalen Musikgesellschaft*, IX, 247.

38. A. Moser, *op. cit.*, p. 73*n*. According to him, Burney's Valentini should be the flutist Roberto Valentini.

39. *Cf.* Piancastelli, *op. cit.*, pp. 62–64, 72. Apropos of Corelli's posthumous elevation to the peerage, see also the correspondence which passed between Ippolito Corelli and the Prince Elector Johann Wilhelm, in A. Einstein, *op. cit.*, p. 422 ff.

40. *Catalogo della mostra Corelliana.*

41. Alberto Cametti, *Arcangelo Corelli, I suoi quadri e i suoi violini*, Rome, 1927.

42. Number 418 of *Musikbücher und Musiker Autographen aus der Sammlung Wilhelm Heyer in Köln*, May 9 and 10, 1927, Liepmannssohn, Berlin.

43. *Dictionnaire historique des musiciens*, Paris, 1810, I, 272. *Cf.* also Francesco Regli, *Storia del Violino in Piemonte*, Turin, 1863, p. 32, and Gerber, *Neues Lexikon*, 1812, p. 798. Vidal, *op. cit.*, II, 114, makes the observation that the culmination of Corelli's talent coincided with that period during which Antonio Stradivarius produced his finest violins.

44. Abbé Raguenet, *op. cit.* p. 16.

45. Letter from T. Dampier to W. Windham on April 4, 1741. Mentioned by J. R. Clemens, "Handel and Carey," *The Sackbut*, January, 1931.

46. This "affair of the fifths" is thoroughly discussed by F. Vatielli, *op. cit.*, pp. 184–88. On this subject see also G. Gaspari, *La Musica in Bologna*, Milan, p. 15, and F. Vatielli, "Le Quinte del Corelli," *Nuova Musica*, Florence, No. 258; L. Busi, *Il Padre G. B. Martini*, Bologna, 1891, pp. 93–102; D'Angeli, in Piancastelli, *op. cit.*, pp. 187–88.

47. "*Ertz-Engel, Ertz-Teuffel*," in the anecdote published by J. G. Walther. Dr. Piancastelli places this meeting in Germany. But Walther's account, the first we have of the incident, tells us that it occurred in Rome whither Strungk had accompanied the Duke Ernst August of Hanover. Fayolle, in his *Notices sur*

Corelli, Paris, 1810, p. 5, copies Walther, rather inaccurately. For N. A. Strungk, *cf.* Mattheson, *Grundlage einer Ehrenpforte*, 1740, pp. 352–54, and especially Fritz Berend, *Nicolaus Adam Strungk*, Hanover, 1913.

48. Hawkins, *op. cit.*, II, 678.

49. Trevisani designed the frontispiece for the *Concerti Grossi*, Opus VI.

50. Laurenti, quoted by Piancastelli, *op. cit.*, p. 72, note 35. To round off the biography of Corelli, I will draw attention to his certain identity with a mysterious personage who is twice encountered in the *Quellen Lexikon* of Eitner: CORRELIDA, *Arcangelico*, see Tusignano (I, 62); TUSIGNANO, *Arcangelico Correlida* (!!).

51. J. Ecorcheville, "La Sonate," an unfinished, unpublished manuscript of 69 pages formerly belonging to Henry Prunières, who made me a present of it in 1933 after the publication of my first work on Corelli.

52. Regarding these Bolognese influences, *cf.* Vatielli, *Il Corelli*, *passim*.

53. Lionel de la Laurencie, *L'Ecole française de violon de Lully à Viotti*, 3 vols., Paris, 1922–1924.

54. S. de Brossard, *Dictionnaire de Musique*, Paris, 1703, *s.v.* "Sonate."

55. On this subject, see Maugars' account, pp. 128–129.

56. As early as 1655 Biagio Marini frequently wrote sonatas in three and four movements. *La Angela* by Marco Uccellini, 1645, had only three. In contrast, Massimiliano Neri, Legrenzi, and Veracini frequently exceed six movements, the slow movements for the most part being reduced to bridge passage formulas of a few measures.

57. *Cf.* W. H. Riehl, *Arcangelo Corelli im Wendepuukte zweier musikgesechichte Epochen*, p. 222.

58. The *Ciacona* of the second book of Corelli runs to exactly 127 measures, the *Passagallo* of Vitali has 262 measures. Even the sonatas of the middle of the century, those of Massimiliano Neri, Tarquinio Merula, Montalbano, and Marini are as developed as the trios of Corelli.

59. And not, as was stated in Vincent d'Indy's *Cours de Composition*, II, 80, the subject only, which Bach is said to have made his countersubject. It is stated also in the *Cours de Composition*, II, 225, that this same countersubject of Corelli had inspired the *Sonata Italiana* of F. W. Rust where it appears in a form both hesitant and blurred. E. Neufeld has discovered (*Revue S.I.M.*, November, 1913) that the original of the elder Rust does not contain any allusion, direct or indirect, to Corelli; it is an interpolation by his ingenious grandson, who has here and there added episodes in this way.

60. Félix Huet, *Etude sur les différentes Ecoles de violon*, Chalons-sur-Marne, 1880, p. 322.

61. Gasparini, *L'Armonico practico al Cimbalo*, 2nd ed., Venice, 1715, p. 44. *Cf.* also Arteaga, *Le Rivoluzioni del Teatro musicale italiano*, 2nd ed., Venice, 1785, II, 24; Avison, *An Essay on Musical Expression*, 3rd ed., London, 1775, p. 83.

62. F. T. Arnold, *The Art of Accompaniment from a Thorough-Bass as Practiced in the 17th and 18th Centuries*, London, 1931, pp. 901–03. For anyone who wishes to study the harmony of Corelli in detail, and particularly his figured bass, pages 805, 824, 825, 903–05 are equally important.

63. *Proceedings of the Musical Association*, 1920–1921.

64. Vincenzio Martinelli, *Lettere familiari e critiche*, London, 1758, pp. 377–81. The letter wherein this passage is found is ad-

dressed to the Duke of Buckinghamshire. The incorrect quotation which I gave in "La Technique du Violon chez les premiers sonatistes français," *Revue S. I. M.*, August–September, 1911, was borrowed from Fayolle, *Notices sur Corelli, Tartini, Gaviniès, Pugnani et Viotti*, Paris, 1810, pp. 8–9.

65. F. Torrefranca, "Arcangelo Corelli" in Piancastelli, *op. cit.*, p. 149.

66. The text of this is given in Piancastelli, *op. cit.*, p. 39.

67. *Cf.* Riehl, *op. cit.*, p. 198.

68. Alfred Heuss, "Die venetianischen Opern-Sinfonien," *Sammelbände der internationalen Musikgesellschaft*, IV, 465.

69. Piancastelli, *op. cit.*, p. 53, quotes the account of Crescimbeni in which it was stated: "Meraviglioso . . . fu l'esatto accordo degli strumenti da fiato con quelli da arco . . . ma cio ch'egli fece col suo strumento eccede la meraviglia stessa. . . ." (Marvelous was the true intonation between wind instruments and strings . . . but that which he produced with his instrument exceeded the marvel itself.)

70. Letter of July 2, 1913, in Piancastelli, *op. cit.*, p. 145.

71. Felipe Pedrell, "Folk-Lore musical castillan du XVIe siècle," in *Sammelbände der internationalen Musikgesellschaft*, I, 387.

72. O. Gombosi, "Zur Frühgeschichte der Folia," *Acta musicologica*, July–December, 1936, p. 119.

73. Paul Nettl, "Zwei spanische Ostinatothemen," *Zeitschrift für Musikwissenschaft*, I, 694. *Cf.* further, apropos "Les Folies d'Espagne," A. Moser, "Zur Genesis der Folies d'Espagne," *Archiv für Musikwissenschaft*, I, 3; R. Mitjana, in *Encyclopédie . . . et Dictionnaire du Conservatoire*, Part I, 2097 and 2103; J. S. Shedlock, in *Sammelbände der internationalen Musikgesellschaft*,

VI, 175 and 418; Dr. Carl Brückner, "La Sarabanda," *La Cultura musicale*, IV, Bologna, 1922; M. Pincherle, in *Revue Musicale*, April, 1923, p. 263; John Ward, "The Folia," a communication submitted to the Congress of the International Society for Musical Research, Utrecht, July, 1952.

74. "Mémoires," in *Revue de Bretagne et Vendée*, 1888, I, 244. *Les Folies d'Espagne* are noted in the "Suite de Dances pour les violons et hautbois qui se jouent ordinairement à tous les bals chez le Roy," *Recueil Philidor*, Bibliothèque Nationale Vm⁷ 3555. They were still considered a dance in 1724, the year in which Lorenz Mizler described them in his *Musikalische Bibliothek*, II, 100: "It is a sort of Sarabande which is nowise high-spirited, but whose ancient melody reveals great beauty though its range does not exceed a fourth." It was also a truly traditional tune. A most improper couplet given by Mme de C . . . (Du Noyer) in her *Lettres historiques*, New edition, 1720, I, 246, carries the simple title, *"Sur l'air des Folies d'Espagne."* As to the variations on this theme composed from 1700 right up to the present day, their list would fill pages and would apply to the violin, harpsichord, pianoforte, flute, harp, guitar, mandolin, lyre, and even the "instrument called the Bissex" for which van Hecke wrote a method about 1780. Dr. Charles van den Borren has pointed out to me numerous uses of the air of *Les Folies d'Espagne* in the French and Flemish songs annotated by van Duyse in *Het oude nederlandsche lied*, Antwerp, 1908, pp. 2600 ff. Spitta mentioned numerous German adaptations for voice of this air ("Sperontes Singende Muse an der Pleisse," *Vierteljahrsschrift für Musikwissenschaft*, 1885). According to Wilhelm Tappert, *Sang und Klang aus alter Zeit*, it was ascribed to a popular Pomeranian, or Swedish theme, or to a *danse macabre* of the Marche country.

75. Chrysander, *G. F. Händel*, 2nd ed., Leipzig, 1919, I, 357.

76. Hubert Le Blanc, *Défense de la basse de Viole*, p. 97.

77. The *Follia* of Sivori, evidence of which has been found in

the programme of one of his concerts at Orleans, dated February 27, 1860 (with César Franck for piano accompaniment!) went beyond the usual plan of this type of composition. A little of Beethoven's Pastoral, Paganini's *Witches Dance,* and an anticipation of *Goyescas* played a part in it, if the wording of the titles is believed:

Folies d'Espagne, performed on the violin by M. Sivori:

Walk of the Masqueraders to the Prado
Village Dance to the Sound of the Pipe
Storm and Prayer
Return of Fine Weather and Repeat of the Dance or Sorcerers' Song

78. C. von Winterfeld quotes a dramatic passage from Monteverdi, dating from 1610, where the violins play in the fifth position, or in the fourth with extension.

79. Regarding the cadence in the old Italian School, *cf.* Heinrich Knödt, "Zur Entwicklungsgeschichte der Kadenzen im Instrumental Konzert," *Sammelbände der internationalen Musikgesellschaft,* April–June 1914. There are rather developed examples in Corelli's Opus I (allegro of the 9th Trio) and Opus III (allegro of the 12th Trio).

80. A. Moser, *Zur Frage der Ornamentik in ihrer Anwendung auf Corelli's Opus V* maintains the unauthenticity of this ornamentation, which could be the work of John Ravenscroft (?). Arnold Schering believes it is authentic ("Zur instrumental Verzierungskunst," *Sammelbände der internationalen Musikgesellschaft,* VII, 366). On this subject consult the specialist works of R. Lach, Goldschmidt, Beyschlag, and Max Kuhn.

81. J. Bonnet, *Histoire de la musique et de ses effets,* 1726, I, 294.

82. *Mémoires de Trévoux,* November, 1735, p. 2365.

83. J. J. Quantz, *Essai d'une méthode pour apprendre à jouer*

de la Flûte traversière, Berlin, 1752, p. 155. Hubert Le Blanc, *op. cit.,* p. 95.

84. The practice of numerous repeats must have been current; in his *Première Elite (Concerti Grossi)* of 1701, Muffat requests that the repeats be performed "in such a way, nevertheless, that the most serious are only played twice in succession; the liveliest airs thrice (with all repeats)." Regarding Pinelli's variations, a catalogue of Hue, about 1745, attributes them to "Signor Petronio."

85. *Op. cit.,* p. 209.

86. *Miscellanea musicale,* Bologna, 1689, p. 45.

87. A. Moser, *Geschichte des Violinspiels,* p. 71.

88. A. Schering, *Geschichte des Instrumentalkonzerts,* 2nd ed., Leipzig, 1927. For this formative period see also P. Magnette, "Notes sur le concerto grosso," *Courrier Musical,* October, 1910; Egon Wellesz, *Die Opern und Oratorien in Wien von 1600–1708,* Vienna, 1919; M. Pincherle "La Naissance du concerto," *Courrier Musical,* October 1, 1930; A. Schering, "Alte Weihnachtssymphonien," *Zeitschrift für Musik,* December 7, 1904; and especially F. Vatielli, "La Genesi del Concerto strumentale e Giuseppe Torelli," *Arte e Vita musicale a Bologna,* 1927.

89. Maugars, *Response faite à un curieux sur le sentiment de la Musique d'Italie escrite à Rome le premier octobre 1639,* republished Thoinan, Paris, 1865, pp. 27–34.

90. G. Muffat, *Ausserlesene mit Ernst und Lust gemengte Instrumental Musik,* Passau, 1701, preface.

91. F. Torrefranca in *Rivista musicale italiana,* July 3, 1917.

92. E. Wright, *Some Observations made in travelling through France, Italy, etc., in the years 1720, 1721 and 1722,* London, 1730, II, 440.

93. *Op. cit.*, II, 332.

94. The libretto of the divertissement by Guidi, which confirms the information given by the *Ragguaglio* in question, has been retrieved by Torrefranca, *loc. cit.* The same details, related in the *Poema* by Guidi published at Verona in 1726, were already known to Burney (III, 551) and Hawkins (II, 674, note 1).

95. Quoted by E. Dent, *op. cit.*, p. 92.

96. It was not rare for composers to take like precautions. Beckmann, in *Das Violinspiel in Deutschland vor 1700*, Leipzig, 1918, p. 10, cites Quagliati's warning to the violinist at the end of the *Sfera armoniosa* (1623) that in the concertante passages he should play the text as written, ornamented solely by trills, and without embroideries; in the same way Grandi, Op. II, 1628, No. 4, orders in a melodic passage "*Sonate come sta*" (play as written).

97. Blainville, *Histoire générale de la Musique*, Paris, 1767, p. 46.

98. *Spectacle de la Nature VII*, Paris, 1747, p. 105.

99. In Grove, 1928, IV, 188. *Cf.* Johann Adam Hiller, *Lebensbeschreibungen*, Leipzig, 1784, p. 183. Hiller mentions not Arcangelo, but a "Joseph Corelli," who is surely Giuseppe Torelli.

100. R. Mitjana, *op. cit.*, Part I, 2187, says: "In the introduction to his technical work, he declares he had lessons from Corelli"; and he refers to *L'Arte y puntual explicacion del modo de tocar el violin*, undated, National Library of Madrid. Curiously enough, the Abbé Laurenti (Piancastelli, *op. cit.*, p. 70, note 16) gives a detailed account of a journey of Corelli in Spain of which no other historian has ever had any inkling.

101. *Cf.* Hawkins, II, 675. This portrait is said to have been painted between 1697 and 1700. H. Bromley, *A Catalogue of Engraved British Portraits*, London, 1793, p. 239, dates Smith's

engraving from 1704. Dr. Piancastelli, *op. cit.*, pp. 116–19, has made a careful study of Corellian iconography. He derives all the portraits of Corelli still extant (that of Trevisani mentioned by the inventory has been lost) either from Howard's, or from the bust placed in the Pantheon, which he attributes to the sculptor Angelo Rossi. There should be added to the copious list which he furnishes an engraving by Des Rochers (Bromley, p. 239), and a painted portrait by an unknown artist belonging to the Royal Society of Musicians (*An Illustrated Catalogue of the Music Loan Exhibition Held at Fishmonger's Hall, June and July, 1904*, London, 1909, p. 228).

A medallion by Giuseppe Romagnoli is reproduced at the end of the work of Dr. Piancastelli. Another, of anonymous origin, cast in England, is cited by Andorfer and Epstein, *Musica in nummis*, Vienna, 1907, No. 684.

102. Burney, III, 556.

103. Francesco Galeazzi, *Elementi teorico–practici di musica*, Rome, 1791, I, 50 and 202.

104. Reported by the Hon. Roger North, *Memoirs of Musick* (1728), Edition Rimbault, London, 1846, p. 130.

105. *Comparaison de la Musique italienne et de la musique françoise*, IV, 229.

106. A. Tamaro, *Nel Giorno della inaugurazione del monumento a Gius. Tartini*, Trieste, 1896, p. 29, thinks that Tartini must have worked with some pupil of Corelli during his stay at Ancona in 1714.

107. *Op. cit.*, pp. 92 and 170.

108. *Notices*, p. 7.

109. *Op. cit.*, II, 89.

110. *Der vollkommene Capellmeister*, Hamburg, 1739, p. 91. Torrefranca, *Origini italiane del Romanticismo musicale*, pp. 302,

316, 337, etc., complains of a systematic silence of the Germans of the eighteenth century vis-à-vis Corelli. In point of fact, he is rarely spoken of; but this could have been unawareness, or been due to the fact that the Germans at that time were absorbed in a style which had slight connection with that of Corelli.

111. In the same way, the "Sarabande" of the *Suites de Pièces pour le clavecin*, IInd book, p. 27, Walsh, 1733, is very closely related to the *follia*. It was seen above that the theme of the *follia* seems always to have been very popular in Germany. To the evidence of Chrysander and Paul Nettl, already mentioned, is joined that of A. Pirro (*J. S. Bach*, p. 200), who detects it in Bach's cantata "Mer hahn en neue Oberkeet," 1742, in the ritornello of aria No. 8 for soprano. It can only be stated that this theme was not entirely mere public property.

112. See "Musical Bibliography."

113. Matthew Locke, in the preface of his *Little Consort of three Parts*, 1656: "I shall make bold to tell them . . . that I never saw any Forain Instrumental Composition (a few French corants excepted) worthy an Englishmans Transcribing . . ." Also, J. Playford, *A Briefe Introduction to the Skill of Musik*, 1654: "Our late and solemn Musick, both Vocal and Instrumental, is now jostled out of esteem by the new Corants and Jigs of Foreigners, to the grief of all sober and judicious Understanders of that formerly solid and good Musick." Evelyn, in his *Diary*, December 21, 1662, derides the introduction into church of 24 violins who play "after ye French fantastical light way, better suiting a tavern or a playhouse than a church. . . ."

114. Cf. Evelyn's *Diary*, March 4, 1656; North, *op. cit.*, p. 99; Cart de Lafontaine, *The King's Musick*, London (1909), pp. 125, 136, 140, 196, 207; C. Stiehl, "Thomas Baltzar," *Monatshefte für Musikgeschichte*, 1888, p. 1.

115. *Op. cit.*, p. 121. Cf. also Evelyn's *Diary*, p. 343; Frank Bridge, "Purcell et Nicola Matteis," *Sammelbände der internationalen Musikgesellschaft*, I (1900), 623.

116. Cf. Van der Straeten, *The Romance of the Fiddle*, London, 1911, p. 117–79. For Needler and Opus VI, see Hawkins, II, 806.

117. *Comparaison*, III, 95.

118. Quoted by Van der Straeten, *op. cit.*, p. 120.

119. Pohl, *Mozart und Haydn in London*, II, Vienna, 1868, pp. 23, 199.

120. H. Prunières, *L'Opéra italien en France avant Lully*, Paris, 1913, *passim*.

121. Séré de Rieux, "La Musique," *Dons des Enfants de Latone*, 1734, p. 112, confirmed later by Daquin, *Letters sur les hommes célèbres*, 1752, I, 129, and Corrette, preface to the *Maître de clavecin*, 1753. Regarding the sonatas of François Couperin, *cf.* Julien Tiersot, "Les Nations, Sonates en trio de François Couperin," in *Revue de Musicologie*, New Series, June 2, 1922.

122. *Op. cit.*, p. 754.

123. Charles Van den Borren, "Tobacco and Coffee in Music," *Musical Quarterly*, July, 1932, p. 367, gives the prelude of the Cantata "Le Caffé," which could have been signed by Corelli.

124. *Cf.*, for example, *La Musique Théorique et Pratique dans son ordre naturel*, Paris, 1722.

125. The sale catalogues of Bourret (1735), De La Boissière (1764), etc., mention Corelli's works almost in their entirety.

126. Léon Vallas, *La Musique à Lyon au XVIIIe siècle*, 1908, I, 18.

127. Hubert Le Blanc, *op. cit.*, p. 6.

128. Published from 1704 to 1706 at Brussels by Foppens, and republished by Bonnet (1724) as a sequel to *L'Histoire de la Musique* of which it forms volumes II, III, and IV.

129. *Op. cit.*, II, 24.

130. *Op. cit.*, pp. 62, 105. I forego citing all Corelli's partisans now that the issue has been decided; the list would be very long and the texts would only reiterate those I have already given.

131. *Op. cit.*, p. 8.

132. *Dissertation sur la Musique françoise et italienne*, by Mr. L'A. P., Amsterdam, 1754, p. 18.

133. Examples are: *Entretiens d'un musicien françois avec un gentilhomme russe sur les Effets de la Musique moderne*, by M. D. (Du Chargey), Dijon, 1773, p. 31: "As to those who have composed symphonies without any other design than to manifest in an agreeable way the effect of vibrations of the sonorous mass of instruments, Corelli holds first place." G. B. Moreschi, *Orazione in lode del Padre Maestro Giamb. Martini*, Bologna, 1786: "Corelli has followed Nature rather than art, Martini has followed both. . . . Corelli moves us to admiration of an almost divine rapture. . . ."

134. Discours Préliminaire to *XII Sonates à Violon seul et Basse* by Corelli, edited by J. B. Cartier, Paris, 1799. By this time, this was an accepted truth. Bossler wrote in 1791: "Broadly speaking, the art of the violin can be likened to a tower, the foundations of which might be said to have been laid by Corelli, which Tartini and the elder Stamitz erected, and which Lolli crowned with its pointed roof." In *Speyersche Realzeitung*, quoted by Mennicke, *Hasse und die Brüder Graun*, Leipzig, 1906, p. 11.

135. *The Story of the Violin*, London, n.d., p. 157.

136. A. Choron, *Principes de Composition des Ecoles d'Italie*, *III*, 1808.

137. Virgile Josz, "Watteau Musicien," *Mercure de France*, December, 1902.

138. Unpublished manuscript. *Cf.* Riehl, p. 197: "Corelli most definitely was no seeker after novelty." Moser, *Geschichte*, p. 71: "Corelli was neither a daring innovator in a composer's role like Monteverdi, nor a violinist's like Biagio Marini."

139. *Op. cit.*

140. Vatielli, *Il Corelli*, p. 181.

141. In *Le Origine italiane del Romanticismo musicale*, 1930, p. 37, Torrefranca goes further. I give his text verbatim: "Già l'arte del Corelli ha dei fervori minuti, dei guizzi improvisi, degli abbandoni spontanei e delle follie accese che indicano il senso nuovo della nuova civiltà che ben puo dirsi musicale: Ricerca intuitiva." (Already Corelli's art has nuances of fervor, unexpected flashes, spontaneously diminished tensions, and glowing extravagances that betoken the new sense of the nascent sensibility which musically might well be called: Intuitive discernment.)

142. The phrase of la Viéville, already quoted, is in the *Comparaison*, II, 55: "Quelle joye, quelle bonne opinion de soi-même n'a pas un homme qui connoît quelque chose au cinquième Opera de Corelli!" (What joy, what a fine opinion of himself has a man who knows something of the fifth Opera of Corelli!) The Abbé Raguenet in his *Defense du Parallèle*, Paris, 1705, p. 50: "Par malheur, mon pauvre Chevalier, Corelli n'a point fait de cinquième Opéra. . . . (Unfortunately, my poor Sir, Corelli has not written any fifth Opera at all.) He harps on the point, pp. 57, 78. Lecerf de la Viéville protests victoriously (IV, p. 201). The worst of it is that more modern writers have made the blunder for which de la Viéville was wrongfully reproached, for example, C. de Brack, in the translation of the *Dissertation sur l'état actuel de la musique en Italie* by Perotti; and A. L. Blondeau, *Histoire de la musique*, II, Paris, 1847.

143. Francesco Pasini, "Notes sur la vie de Gio. Batt. Bassani," *Sammelbände der internationalen Musikgesellschaft*, VII, 581.

VI

Musical Bibliography

*Violino primo (secondo, etc.)./Sonate/a trè, doi Violini, e
Violone o Arcileuto,/col Basso per l'Organo./Consecrate/alla
Sacra Real Maesta di/Cristina Alessandra/Regina di Svezia, etc./
Da Arcangelo Corelli da Fusignano,/detto il Bolognese,/Opera
Prima./In Roma, Nella Stamperia di Gio. Angelo Mutij 1681. Con
licenza de' Super./* (In —4°, Library, Liceo Musicale, Bologna)

Apart from the collected editions of Walsh and Cooke (London, *ca.* 1710 and 1732), the Trio Sonatas of Corelli were published in separate parts.

Bologna, Giacomo Monti, 1682.
Rome, undated (1683).
Bologna, Monti, at the expense of Mario Silvani, 1684.
Venice, Gioseppe Sala, 1684.
Modena, Antonio Vitaliani, 1685.
Rome, Mascardi, 1685.
Bologna, Monti, 1688.
Antwerp, Henrico Aertssens, 1688.
Rome, Angelo Mutij, 1688.
Bologna, Silvani, 1697.
Bologna, unnamed, 1698.
Amsterdam, Estienne Roger, undated, No. 241 (*ca.* 1695–1700).
Bologna, Silvani, 1704.
Bologna, Monti, 1704.
Venice, Gioseppe Sala, 1707.

Paris, Ribou, undated (*ca.* 1700–1710).

London, Walsh and Hare, undated (*ca.* 1710).

Amsterdam, E. Roger and M. C. Le Cène, undated (*ca.* 1715).

OPUS II

Violino primo (violino secondo, etc.)./Sonate da Camera/A trè, doi Violini, e Violone, o Cimbalo/consecrate/All' Emin^mo e Rev^mo Signore/il Signor/Card. Panfilio/Da Arcangelo Corelli da Fusignano,/Detto il Bolognese,/Opera seconda./In Roma, Nella stamperia di Gio; Angelo Mutii. 1685. Con licenza de Sup./(In —4°, Library, Liceo Musicale, Bologna)

Bologna, Monti, 1685.

Modena, Vitaliani, 1685.

Venice, Gioseppe Sala, 1686.

Venice, Gioseppe Sala, 1687.

Bologna, Silvani, 1688.

Rome, Angelo Mutij, 1688.

Antwerp, Aertssens, 1689.

Rome, Mascardi, 1691.

Venice, Gioseppe Sala, 1692.

Bologna, Monti, 1694.

Amsterdam, Estienne Roger, undated (*ca.* 1695).

Venice, Sala, 1697.

Bologna, Silvani, 1701.

Rome, Komarek, 1701.

Venice, Sala, 1705.

Paris, Ribou, undated (*ca.* 1700–1710).

London, Walsh, undated (*ca.* 1703).

Amsterdam, Roger et Le Cène, undated (*ca.* 1715?).

OPUS III

Violino primo (secondo, etc.)/Sonate à tre, doi Violini, e Violone, o Arcileuto/col Basso per l'Organo/Consecrate all'/

Altezza Ser^ma di Francesco II. Duca/di Modena, Reggio etc./da Arcangelo Corelli da Fusignano detto il Bolognese/Opera Terza/ in Roma per Gio. Giacomo Komarek Boemo con licenza de sup. 1689./(In —4°, Collection Piancastelli)

A manuscript of this opus III, presumably an autograph, forms part of the Piancastelli collection, Biblioteca Communale A. Saffi, Forli.

Modena, eredi Soliani, 1689.

Bologna, Monti, 1689.

Venice, Sala, 1691.

Antwerp, Henri Aertssens, 1691 (Catalogue Henning Oppermann, No. 421, Basle, 1931).

Bologna, Monti, 1695.

Rome, Mascardi, 1695.

Amsterdam, Estienne Roger, undated (*ca.* 1700).

Bologna, Silvani, 1702.

Venice, Sala, 1710.

London, Walsh, undated (*ca.* 1700–1710).

OPUS IV

Violino Primo (secondo, etc.)/Sonate à tre composte per l'Accademia dell' Em^mo e Rev^mo Sig^r Cardinale Otthoboni/et all' Eminenza sua consecrate/da Arcangelo Corelli da Fusignano/Opera quarta,/In Roma per Gio. Giacomo Komarek Boemo Con licenza de Sup. 1694/ (In —4°, Library, Liceo Musicale, Bologna)

Bologna, P. M. Monti, 1694.

Venice, Sala, 1695.

Rome, Komarek, 1695.

Amsterdam, Roger et Delorme, 1696.

Rome and Modena, Rosati, 1697.

Bologna, Silvani, 1698.

Venice, Sala, 1701.

London, Walsh and Hare (1701–1702).

Bologna, Silvani, 1704.

Venice, Sala, 1710.

Paris, Boivin, undated (*ca.* 1720).

Nuremberg, at the expense of G. M. Endters, undated (*ca.* 1730?).

OPUS V

Parte prima (*seconda*)/*Sonate a Violino e Violone o Cimbalo/ Dedicate all Altezza Serenissima Elettorale di/Sofia Carlotta/ Elettrice di Brandenburgo/Principessa di Brunswich et Luneburgo Duchessa di/Prussia e di Magdeburgo Cleves Giuliers Berga Stetino/Pomerania Cassubia e de Vandali in Silesia Crossen/ Burgravia di Norimberg Principessa di Halberstatt/Minden e Camin Contessa di Hohenzollern e/Ravenspurg Ravenstain Lauenberg e Buttau/Da Arcangelo Corelli da Fusignano/Opera quinta/ Incisa da Gasparo Pietra Santa/*. Without name of publisher or date (the dedication is dated January 1, 1700), fol. obl. in score.

Rome, same edition, 1700, with the announcement "*Si vendono a Pasquino all'Insegna della stella da Filippo Farinelli.*"

Amsterdam (Estienne Roger?), 1700. The announcement of the *London Gazette* hereafter cited mentions an edition which had already appeared at Amsterdam. Perhaps this is the same which is given at the end of the first edition of the *Histoire des Sévarambes,* published by Estienne Roger in 1702.

London, Walsh, August, 1700 (announced in the *London Gazette* of August 26th–29, 1700, according to E. Van der Straeten, *The Romance of the Fiddle,* p. 177).

London, Walsh, January, 1701.

Paris, Foucault, undated (*ca.* 1701).

Venice, Zatta, undated (*ca.* 1705).

Amsterdam, Estienne Roger (*ca.* 1706).

Paris, Massard de la Tour, 1708.

Paris, Ballard, 1708.

Rouen, Cassone, 1709 (permission to print renewed in 1719 and 1729).

Amsterdam, Estienne Roger, published "with the ornaments," 1710–1711.

Amsterdam, Mortier, undated (*ca.* 1711).

Bologna, gli eredi del Silvani, 1711.

London, Walsh, with the ornaments, 1711.

Amsterdam, Estienne Roger, "latest edition" (*ca.* 1710).

Amsterdam, Estienne Roger, third edition, "with the ornaments" (*ca.* 1715).

Amsterdam, Estienne Roger, published in separate parts (*ca.* 1715).

London, Daniel Wright, 1717.

Paris, Ballard, 1719.

London, R. Meares (*ca.* 1720).

London, Benjamin Cooke (*ca.* 1735).

Paris, Ch. N. Le Clerc, 1736.

London, J. Walsh (*ca.* 1740).

London, Johnson (*ca.* 1750).

Paris, Le Clerc, 1765.

London, R. Birchall (*ca.* 1770?).

Madrid, unnamed, May, 1772 (No. 773 of Liepmannssohn Catalogue No. 154).

Florence, Ranieri del Vivo (1777).

Paris, La Chevardière, "Last edition engraved by Me Leclair"; this is the reprint of the Le Clerc edition (*ca.* 1771).

Paris, Sieber, undated (*ca.* 1780).

Naples, Marescalchi (*ca.* 1790).

Paris, Le Duc, "latest edition," undated (*ca.* 1790).

Paris, Petit, undated (?).

Paris, Janet et Cotelle, edited by J. B. Cartier, 1799.

London, J. Dale and Sons (*ca.* 1800).

Vienna, nel Magazin della Cäs. Real priv. Stamperia Chimica, 1804.

London, Preston (*ca.* 1815).

London, Goulding d'Almaine (*ca.* 1815).

London, Bland and Weller (*ca.* 1815).
London, A. Hamilton (*ca.* 1815).
Paris, Gambaro (?).
London, Clementi, with a thorough Bass for the pianoforte by
Muzio Clementi, undated (*ca.* 1815 ?).

OPUS VI

*Concerti grossi/con duoi Violini e Violoncello di Concertino
obligati e duoi/altri Violini, Viola e Basso di Concerto Grosso ad
arbitrio,/che si potranno radoppiare;/dedicati all'/Altezza Serenissima Elettorale/di/Giovanni Guglielmo/Principe Palatino del
Reno; Elettore e Arci-Mares-cialle del Sacro Romano Impero;
Duca di Baviera, Giuliers,/Cleves e Berghe; Principe di Murs;
Conte di/Veldentz, Spanheim, della Marca e/Ravenspurg, Signore
di/Ravenstein, etc., etc., etc./Da Arcangelo Corelli da Fusignano/
Opera Sesta./A Amsterdam/chez Estienne Roger, Marchand Li-
braire/n° 197.*

The publication of the *Concerti Grossi*, Opus VI, raises a rather
curious problem. Hawkins and Burney, followed by Eitner and
Schering, date the publication from 1712. But we have seen that
Corelli in his will entrusted to Matteo Fornari the task of publishing this Opus VI. The construction put on the phrase of Corelli
could be challenged; but doubt vanishes in the light of the dedicatory epistle by Fornari, dated from Rome, the 20th of November, 1714, appearing in the edition which for a long time was erroneously thought to be the second:

"May V. A. E. (Your Highness the Elector) allow this work,
which was dedicated to You by Arcangelo Corelli, the composer,
during his lifetime, to be presented to V. A. E. by me on coming
from the press after Corelli's death; and in this wise will be ful-
filled his wish that the aforesaid work should have the favour of
your name and patronal privilege. . . ." But there is more to it;
the correspondence between Count Fede and the Prince Elector
Johann Wilhelm on the one hand, and between the Prince and

Fornari on the other, which Dr. Alfred Einstein published (*op. cit.*, pp. 421–22) makes clear the conditions on which Corelli had negotiated with Stefano Ruggieri, the publisher of Amsterdam, to whom the actual execution of the work was to be entrusted. Ruggieri had promised Corelli 150 copies as soon as the printing was completed, which was to be done during the course of 1713; the composer being dead, the promised copies accrued to the benefit of his heir (Fornari). On December 24, 1714, Matteo Fornari announced to the Prince the publication of Opus VI, and the dispatch forthwith of a copy to him; the Prince acknowledged receipt of this very much later, on June 30, 1715.

So the priority of the 1714 edition cannot be doubted. How, if this is so, can the edition be explained which dates, as we are told, from 1712?

An examination of the copy at the Brussels Conservatoire (No. 7287), thanks to Dr. Charles Van Den Borren, shows that the date is given only in the dedicatory epistle, signed by Corelli at Rome on December 3, 1712. This date itself assures us that the edition could not have appeared before the end of 1712, the distance separating Rome and Amsterdam and the time necessary for production presenting an absolute obstacle to this. Furthermore, even if the number of the edition is the same (197), it was Estienne Roger *only* who brought out Fornari's edition; the other printing bears the address "Estienne Roger, Marchand libraire et Michel Charles Le Cène." This latter edition, then, is subsequent to the former edition, and must date from 1715–1720. The different dedications may be explained in several equally plausible ways; either Fornari, who was very obsequious toward Prince Johann Wilhelm, as we have seen, wished to give greater weight to his own dedicatory letter by suppressing the one which Corelli had prepared; or the publisher of Amsterdam, who was the actual recipient of Corelli's letter, saw no point in adding it to Fornari's in the first edition, and utilized it on the occasion of a fresh impression, which thus took on the character of novelty; or, in order to reprint Opus VI as he liked, without negotiating with Fornari, Roger improvised a dedication by Corelli. The action has nothing about it which would have been flatly impossible in Amsterdam in 1715, and the grandiloquence of the dedication tends to add weight to such surmise.

The editions of Opus VI may then be enumerated as follows:

Amsterdam, Estienne Roger, undated (1714). This edition was announced in London in *The Post Man* of December 30, 1714, by Henri Riboteau, agent for the Estienne Roger publications.

Amsterdam, Estienne Roger and M. C. Le Cène, undated (*ca.* 1715–1720).

London, Walsh, undated (1715).

London, Walsh, in score, arrangement by Dr. Pepusch, with a transposed viola part, undated (*ca.* 1732).

Paris, Charles Nicolas Le Clerc (*ca.* 1736).

London, Benjamin Cooke, in score, arrangement of Dr. Pepusch, undated (*ca.* 1730–1740).

London, John Johnson, undated (*ca.* 1745).

London, Preston, undated.

COLLECTED EDITIONS OF OPERA I TO IV

Amsterdam, Estienne Roger, undated (before 1700). These works appear under the title, *Opera prima, sonate a 3, opera seconda, baletti a 3, opera tertia (sic) sonate a 3, opera quarta, baletti a 3* in the catalogue printed by Roger at the end of *Amusements sérieux et comiques* by Rivière et Dufresny, Amsterdam, 1700.

Amsterdam, Estienne Roger, second edition, undated (1705). Announced in the course of a discussion between Nicolini Haym and J. Walsh in *The Post Man*, September, 1705 (W. C. Smith, *op. cit.*, p. 57).

London, Walsh and Hare, 1705.

Amsterdam, Pierre Mortier, undated (*ca.* 1710).

Amsterdam, Estienne Roger, "dernière édition à laquelle on a ajouté le portrait de feu M. Arcangelo Corelli. Cette édition est de la dernière beauté et corrigée avec beaucoup d'exactitude et coute f. 20. 0." Before 1716, catalogue printed at the end of *L'Histoire des Sévarambes*, 2nd ed. II, Amsterdam, 1716.

London, Richard Meares, undated (*ca.* 1710).

London, Benjamin Cooke (*ca.* 1728).

London, Benjamin Cooke, 2nd ed. (*ca.* 1732).

London, Daniel Wright, undated (*ca.* 1732).

London, *The Score of the four operas*, etc., by Dr. Pepusch, Walsh, undated (*ca.* 1735).

Paris, Charles N. Le Clerc, 1736.

Paris, Charles N. Le Clerc, 1750.

London, John Johnson (*ca.* 1750).

London, Bremner (*ca.* 1765).

Paris, Charles N. Le Clerc, 1765.

London, L. R. Cocks, undated.

London, Preston, undated.

London, Harrison (*ca.* 1785).

London, Longman and Broderip (*ca.* 1800).

MISCELLANEOUS WORKS

The essence of Corelli's work lies, as we have said, in his Opera I to VI. But the bibliographies are encumbered with a host of other titles into which we shall seek to introduce a little order, first eliminating ascriptions which are patently erroneous: to give but one example, the *Suonate a 4 violini e fagotti*, Vm⁷ 1109, listed in the catalogue of the Bibliothèque Nationale, are no more than the trios of Opus III bound up with and following the sonatas of Zumbach for strings and bassoons.

We shall list first the transcriptions made of Opera I to VI, and then the manuscript or printed works which, with more or less plausibility, have been attributed to Corelli.

TRANSCRIPTIONS AND ARRANGEMENTS OF OPUS I

Twelve sonatas for the Harpsichord or Organ with accompaniments, London, Harrison, undated (*ca.* 1785). British Museum *Catalogue of Printed Music*, by W. Barclay Squire, I, 304.

6 Sonatas, op. 1 adapted for the organ and 6 Sonatas op. 2 adapted for piano or harpsichord by E. Miller, London, Longman and Broderip (*ca.* 1800). A corresponding volume for Opus III and Opus IV. (Catalogue, William Reeves, No. 77. 1934.)

(*Ib.* after the Sarabande of the 5th trio) *Maggy and Jenny both do undo me. A favourite minuet for two voices, german flutes or other Instr.* London, undated (*ca.* 1735).

OPUS II

(Gavotte from 1st trio) *Advice to Fanny, set for two voices, german flutes or other instr.* London, undated (*ca.* 1730).

(*Ib.* Gavotte) *The Complainant, a song to an air of Corelli.* London, undated (*ca.* 1740).

(11th Trio, Gigue) *Madam, Old Homer, a song to Miss B–y P–tle–aite.* London, *The London Magazine*, 1756.

OPUS III

F. GEMINIANI. *VI Concerti grossi composti delle Sei Sonate del Opera Terza d'A. Corelli.* London, Walsh, 1735.

These are transcriptions of trios 1, 3, 4, 9, 10, and 11 from Corelli's Opus III, for two violins, viola, and violoncello as concertino, and two violins and bass ripieni.

ANTONIO TORELLI (violoncellist, 1686–1765). *Corelli transformato in quattro Antifone ed otto Tantum ergo a varie voci cavati dalla Terza e Quart'opera per indurre li studenti ad un'ottima esecuzione si del suono, che del canto.* (Manuscript, Library, Estense, Modena)

OPUS IV

10th Trio, *A celebrated Gavot.* London, R. Falkener, undated (*ca.* 1775).

OPUS V

A collection of Choice Sonatas, or Salo's (sic) *for a Violin and a Bass,* by Bassani, Corelli, etc. London, Walsh and Hare, 1701.
The 2nd part of Corelli's fifth opera, proper for the harpsicord. London, Walsh and Hare, 1703.

F. GEMINIANI. *XII Concerti grossi . . . composti dell'Sei Soli della prima (seconda) parte dell'Opera quinta d'Arcangelo Corelli.* London, Walsh, undated (*ca.* 1735). Same orchestration as the transcription of Opus III.

Six Solos for a Flute and Bass . . . being the second part of his fifth operas. London, J. Walsh and Hare, 1702.

Two Concertos being the first and eleventh solos of . . . A. Corelli as they are made into concerto by Mr. Obadiah Shuttleworth. London, Joseph Hare (1725 ?).

Id., Nos. 6 and 11 (1702 ?).

A Celebrated Jigg. London, R. Falkener (1770 ?). Gigue from the 5th sonata.

Follia, cf. Chapter II.

A new edition of Corelli's celebrated Solos arranged for the Pianoforte, Organ, etc., by Charles Czerny. London, R. Cocks and Co., 1859.

OPUS VI

Six concertos for two Flutes and a Bass, with a Through Bass for the Harpsicord, Neatly transpos'd from ye great Concertos. London, Walsh and Hare (1730?). Arrangements from the *Concerti Grossi,* Opus VI.

Corelli's celebrated eighth concerto . . . *adapted for the Organ, Harpsichord or Piano Forte by T. Billington op. IX.* Printed for Mr. Billington, London (1790?); arrangement of the 8th concerto of Opus VI.

Bacchus assist us to sing thy great glory. For two voices, german flutes or other Instr^ts. London (1740?); arrangement of the minuet of the 10th concerto.

J. SNOW. *Variations for the Harpsichord to a Minuet of Corellis,* 1760; arrangement of the minuet of the 10th concerto.

Corelli's Concerto composed for the celebration of the Nativity. London, The *Pianoforte Magazine,* VII, No. 2 (1799); arrangement of the 8th concerto.

OTHER ARRANGEMENTS

Some fragments of various arrangements of Corelli appear in:
DOMENICO CORRI, *A Select Collection of Choice Music for the Harpsichord or Piano-Forte*. Composed by Staes, Jomelli, Haydn, Corelli. Edinburgh, Corri and Sutherland, undated.

Philomusicus. Medulla Musicae, being a choice collection of airs. Extracted from the works of Corelli, Bomporti, Torelli, Tibaldi, etc. London, T. Cluer, undated (*ca.* 1727).

J. MARSH. *Select movements from the different works of Corelli, adapted as voluntaries or pieces for the organ*, London, Preston, undated (1806). Liepmannssohn Catalogue, No. 157, and Bibliothèque Pleyel.

Suittes (sic) pour le Clavecin composées à un Clavecin, un Violon et Basse de Viole, ou de Violon ad libitum par Arcangelo Corelli et autres autheurs. Livre premier (et second). A Amsterdam chez Estienne Roger, marchand libraire, undated (Nos. 402 and 403 of the publisher Estienne Roger). These two books contain, among other pieces whose identification is not always easy, numerous movements from Corelli's Opus V: *Sarabanda* of the 7th sonata, *Gavotta* of the 9th, the *follia*, etc. They present great interest from the point of view of the arrangement in that the part for the keyboard is fully realized, as in the *Suites* of Dieupart and the *Pièces de clavecin en concerts* of Rameau.

CORELLI. *Six Setts of Aires for two Flutes and a Bass, being the Choisest of his Preludes, Almands, etc. . . . . Collected out of his several opera's. Transpos'd and fitted to ye Flute, with ye Approbation of our most eminent Masters*, London, J. Walsh and Hare, 1702.

The catalogues of Estienne Roger of Amsterdam mention, prior to 1700:

8 Sonates à 2 flutes, 6 de M. Roger, 1 de M. Paisible et 1 de M. Arcangelo Corelli. This appeared later as No. 339 in Estienne Roger's catalogue issued about 1716; there it specifies that these sonatas are for 2 flutes without bass. To this was added between

1700 and 1706 *XII Sonates de M. Arcangelo Corelli, 6 à 2 flutes et 1 basse continue et 6 à 1 flute et 1 basse continue.* (No. 134 of Estienne Roger.)

The music library of the chateau of Roudnice (Czechoslovakia), belonging to the Lobkowicz family, contains the 2nd and 3rd volumes of this series: *VI Sonates de M. Arcangelo Corelli Tirez de tous ses ouvrages et Transportez pour deux Flûtes et B. C. Livre second. A Amsterdam chez Estienne Roger . . . et Michel Charles Le Cène,* No. 239; and *XII Sonates* (same title) . . . *livre troisième, à Amsterdam, chez Jeanne Roger,* No. 431. *Livre second, contenant six sonates à deux Flûtes et Basse.* (No. 239 of Estienne Roger.)

Pirated edition by Walsh and Hare, London, 1707, under the title *Six Sonata's for 2 Flutes and a Bass, by Arcangelo Corelli, collected out of the choicest of his works, and carefully Transpos'd and contriv'd for 2 Flutes and a Bass.* (*The Post Man,* June 21, 1707.)

By the same publishers:

Choice Italian and English Musick for two Flutes (operatic airs) *to which are added Three excellent new Sonata's and a Chacoone by Corelli Nicolini Haym Torelli and Pez* (announcement in the *Daily Courant,* March 31, 1709).

A Sonata for Two Violins and a thorow Bass with a Trumpet part by Arcangelo Corelli, London, Walsh and Hare, 1704 (*The Post Man,* April 27, 1704).

A Solo in A for a Violin by Arcangelo Corelli. The Solo proper for the Harpsicord or Spinett. London, Walsh and Hare (*ca.* 1704). (Library of Durham Cathedral)

Six select Solos for a Violin and a thorough Bass, collected out of the choicest works of Six Eminent Masters, viz. Signior Martino Betty (Bitti), *Mr. Nicola jun.* (Matteis), *Signior Corelli, etc.* London, Walsh and Hare, 1706. (*Daily Courant* of November 23, 1706)

Finally, Roger's catalogue of 1716 lists as No. 277, *Six sonates de MM. Corelli, Caldara, et Gabrielli à quatre, cinq et six instruments.*

ARRANGEMENTS AND MODERN TRANSCRIPTIONS

Important bibliographical data will be found in:

R. Eitner. *Verzeichniss neuer Ausgaben alter Musikwerke.* Berlin, 1871, p. 77.

J. Peyrot. "Des éditions de musique de chambre instrumentale ancienne en France," *Courrier Musical,* September 1, 1911, pp. 564–65.

British Museum. Catalogue of Music. Accessions, part XI, p. 104.

MANUSCRIPTS OR PRINTED WORKS ATTRIBUTED TO CORELLI

SONATAS FOR VIOLIN AND BASS

Sonatas IV and V of the collection *Sonate a Violino Solo col B. C. composte da Arcangelo Corelli e altri autory et Dediés à M. David Rudgers Courtier à Amsterdam par Estienne Roger.* (Library of the University of Upsala, Caps. 447)

30.

Sonata IV

Allegro C—Adagio C
Allegro C—Largo 3/2
Allegro 6/8

This sonata with the same attribution exists in manuscript form in the Nationalbibliothek, Vienna, No. 31; see Dr. Robert Haas, *Die Estensischen Musikalien,* Regensburg, 1927, p. 90:

31.

Sonata V, Grave

Grave C—Allegro C
Adagio 3/2—Allegro 12/8

This sonata figures also at the beginning of the collection of *Sonate a Violino e Violoncello di Vari Autori,* of which the copy belonging to the library of the Liceo Musicale of Bologna is probably unique. The collection contains, after that of Corelli, six other sonatas by Torelli, Montanari, Giacomo Perdieri (Predieri?), Carlo Mazolini, Giuseppe Jachini, and Clemente Rozzi. This undated work is, according to Vatielli, of Bolognese printing. The collection of Amsterdam is prior to 1700. In fact, it appears in the catalogue of Estienne Roger printed at the end of *Amusements sérieux et comiques,* dated 1700.

Dr. R. Haas, p. 123, also draws attention to a *Sonatta à Violino Solo* in the Este collection which could be attributed to Corelli:

32.

SONATAS FOR OBOE, VIOLINS AND BASS

Haas, pp. 168–69, also mentions two sonatas in manuscript for four parts—Oboe, Violins I & II, and Bass—under the title *Sonata con Aboe (sic) e Violini.*

33.

34.

The opening of the second one does recall a transposition of the first sonata of publication No. 198 of Estienne Roger, *Sonate a tre . . . ouvrage posthume*, which begins thus:

35.

TRIOS

Besides the four fundamental collections of trios, Opus I to IV, engraved and often reprinted in Corelli's lifetime, the old publishers have attributed some others to him. It seems impossible to determine the degree of authenticity of these. First there are the (*VI*) *Sonate a tre, Due Violini Col Basso par* (*sic*) *l'organo Di Arcangelo Corelli da Fusignano Ouvrage posthume a Amsterdam chez Estienne Roger* (No. 198). The edition must date from 1714–1716. It appears in the catalogue of Estienne Roger in *L'Histoire des Sévarambes* (*ca.* 1716).

Their style is candidly very Corellian. What would tend to confirm the attribution is the fact that two of the trios, the 5th and the 6th, appear in a manuscript collection preserved in the Biblioteca Nazionale of Turin (Raccolta "Renzo Giordano") under the title *Sinfonie a 3. di A. Corelli*, of which ten other pieces, duly authenticated, belong to Opera I to IV.

36.

37.

Then comes a collection which is very similar as to style:
XII Sonata's, In three Parts For two Violins a Bass, with a Through Bass for the Organ or Harpsichord. Opera 7th. London, R. Bremner, undated (*ca.* 1765).

Next, and differing from the two preceding publications, there are:
XII Sonatas for Two Violins and Violoncello with a Thorough Bass for the Harpsichord. The Author unknown but supposed by several Eminent Masters . . . to be . . . A. Corelli. London, J. Johnson (*ca.* 1755).

For further mention:
Corellis Posthumous Works, announced by Walsh and Hare in *The Post Man* of November 6, 1718.
Sonatos (sic) for two Violins, a Violoncello and thro' Bass; by Arcangelo Corelli; being his Posthumous Work, or 7th Opera. London, Walsh and Hare, 1719. (*Post Boy* of February 26, 1719)

The *Catalogo della Mostra Corelliana* (see Bibliography) lists as No. 132 an eighteenth-century manuscript in the library of San Pietro a Majella at Naples, entitled: *Libro di Partiture delle quattro Mute, di Sonate a 3, due da Chiesa* (manuscript copies of the first four works of Corelli), *con l'aggiunte anche di alcune altre Sonate del medemo (sic) Autore, che non son date alle stampe.* The *aggiunte* (addition) in question comprises 3 sonatas. The first for two violins and trumpet offers in its opening phase some analogy with the first two sonatas of the posthumous set, No. 198, of Estienne Roger; the finale is preceded by a short trumpet solo with figured bass. The second is identical with the 7th of the posthumous set. The third, in four parts (*2 violini, violetta e basso*) is not found anywhere else.

Besides these works of more or less doubtful authenticity, reference must be made to an odd apocryphal collection exposed some time ago by our late confrere, F. T. Arnold of Bath, in an article entitled: "A Corelli Forgery," *Proceedings of the Musical Associa-*

tion (*London*), *Forty-seventh Session*, 1920–21. It concerns the *Suonate da camera a tre . . . da Arcangelo Corelli . . . Opera quarta, Prima Parte. Nuovamente ristampata. In Anversa, da Henrico Aertssen, 1692.* (British Museum, g. 40)

The mere wording of the title is quite amazing. How could a publisher of Antwerp *ristampare* (reprint) in 1692 an Opus IV when, from all the evidence, the first edition of Opus IV did not appear till 1694? The contents are not such as to throw any more light on the matter. They differ completely from the text of the genuine Opus IV (the text of which the same publisher, Aertssen of Antwerp, was to issue in 1695 under the title of *Academia Ottobonica overo Suonate a tre instrumenti . . . Opera quarta*). In vain has F. T. Arnold sought to identify the true composer of the pseudo Opus IV of 1692, in which several singularities of technique show up the imposture. To mention just one: the chain of *eleven* movements of the fourth trio: *Preludio* (*grave*), *Allemanda* (*allegro mà suave*), *Baletto francese* (*allegro*), *Ghiga* (*presto*), *Sarabanda* (*presto!*), *Brando* (*largo*), *Minuet* (*allegro*), *Borea* (*prestissimo*), *Chiusa* (*adagio*). Attempts to ascribe the work to Giovanni Battista Vitali, to Torelli, and to Bassani have come to naught.

Finally, Gerber's *Neues historisch-biographisches Lexikon* (1812, I, 788) mentions among the doubtful works a set of 9 trios engraved at Amsterdam by Le Cène with the list number of Opus VII; this would be the reprint of Ravenscroft's trios which were published at Rome in 1695. Gerber's comment corroborates a passage from Hawkins (II, 678), which runs: "Ravenscroft professed to imitate Corelli in those sonatas which Roger published and tried to make the world believe were some of the earliest of his works."

A copy of the *soi-disant* Opus VII which I have been able to examine in the music library of the chateau of Roudnice confirms Gerber. It throws into relief Le Cène's fraudulent intention; by his manner of arranging the title he was careful to obliterate his reservations, so discreetly hinted at, as to the authenticity of the work. In actual fact, the name of Corelli stands out in enormous characters in the middle of the title:

Sonate a trè Doi Violini è Basso per il Cimbalo Si crede siano state composte di

ARCANGELO CORELLI

avanti le sue altre opere. Amsterdam. Stampate à spese di Michel Carlo Le Cène.

These are indeed the sonatas of Ravenscroft, but the number of the publication (No. 566) proves that it was a case of a very belated reprint, done after 1730 and probably undertaken unbeknown to the actual composer.

CONCERTOS

An unpublished concerto grosso in *g* in eight parts is located in the library of Gesellschaft der Musikfreunde at Vienna.

The Nationalbibliothek at Vienna has in the Este collection (No. 120, referred to by Haas, *op. cit.*, p. 183) another concerto which is very odd. In its orchestration—*Violino Primo Principale, 2 Trombe o Violini, Violoncello, Basso*—it verges on the concerto for soloist, although the sagacity of the passage work, and the narrow compass of the tessitura of the principal part, which does not go beyond the third position, are in the spirit of the concerto grosso. It comprises three movements: *Allegro (C), Grave, Presto.* But the middle movement is only indicated by the expression *Grave tacet* over the ripieni parts. No doubt it was written, according to contemporary usage, for principal violin and figured-bass on a single sheet of score, which may have disappeared.

The theme of the *Allegro:*

38.

evokes Vivaldi, in particular manuscript No. CX.1076 in the Landesbibliothek at Dresden, and also Albinoni, Opus V, No. 3, *allegro:*

39.

Finally, we should mention Corelli's name as figuring in a collection of *6 sonates de MM. Corelli, Caldara et Gabrieli à 4, 5 et 6 parties* announced in 1702 in the catalogue printed in *Histoire des Sévarambes*, 1st ed., by Estienne Roger among the "Sonates à fortes parties," an appellation with which at this period he designated concertos and symphonies. The same collection appears in the catalogue of 1715–1716 as No. 277.

VOCAL MUSIC

A *Veni Sancte Spiritus* in manuscript, attributed to Corelli, in the library of Yale University.

A *Missa choralis*, also attributed to Corelli, in the National-bibliothek at Vienna.

VII

Bibliography

With rare exceptions only books or articles especially devoted to Corelli appear in this bibliography, to the exclusion of references appearing in histories of the violin or in general works.

As to authors often cited in abbreviations in the text of the book, the quotations from Burney are from the 2nd ed. of *A General History of Music*, London, 1789; those from Hawkins are from the posthumous edition in two volumes of *A General History of the Science and Practice of Music*, London, 1853. Those of Lecerf de la Viéville are from the *Comparaison de la musique italienne et de la musique françoise*, republished to supplement *L'Histoire de la musique et de ses effets* by Bonnet-Bourdelot (1726) of which it forms the last three volumes. II signifies the second volume of the set, III the third, and not the 2nd and 3rd parts of the *Comparaison*.

Arnold, F. T. "A Corelli Forgery," *Proceedings of the Musical Association*, 47th session, 1920–1921.

Barblan, Guglielmo. *Un musicista trentino, Francesco A. Bonporti*, Florence, 1940.

Berlioz, Hector. "Corelli," *Revue et Gazette musicale*, June 25, 1837.

Bingley, W. *Musical Biography*, London, 1834.

Bukofzer, Manfred. *Music in the Baroque Era*, New York, 1947.

Cametti, Alberto. "Arcangelo Corelli à Saint-Louis-des-Français à Rome," *Revue Musicale*, January, 1922.

———. *Arcangelo Corelli, I suoi quadri e i suoi violini*. Rome, 1927.

Conrat, H. J. "Archangelo Corelli," *Allgemeine Musikzeitung*, 1903, p. 481.

Crescimbeni. "Arcangelo Corelli," *Notizie istoriche degli Arcadi morti*, I, Rome, 1720.

Deas, Stewart. "Arcangelo Corelli," *Music and Letters*, January, 1953.

Della Corte, A. "Corelli a Napoli," *Il Giornale*, August 1, 1953.

Diem, Nelly. "Der Geiger Arcangelo Corelli," *Neue Musikzeitung*, 1918.

Engel, Carl. *Das Instrumentalkonzert*, Leipzig, 1932.

Eximeno, D. A. *Dell'origine e delle regole della musica*, Rome, 1774.

Farini, P. "Biografia di Arcangelo Corelli," *Biografie e ritratti di XXIV illustri romagnoli*, Forli, 1835.

Fayolle, François. *Notices sur Corelli, Tartini, Gaviniès, Pugnani et Viotti*, Paris, 1810; translated into German in the *Allgemeine musikalische Zeitung*, June 19, 1811. There is also a Swedish translation, *Om Violinens Ursprung, jemte biografiska anteckningar öfver Corelli*, Stockholm, 1811.

Fétis, F. J. "Corelli," *Galerie des Musiciens célèbres*, II, Paris, 1827.

Galli, A. "Arcangelo Corelli," *La musica popolare*, Milan, June, 1882.

Giazotto, Remo. *Tomaso Albinoni*, Milan, 1945.

Hawkins, Sir John. "The General History and Peculiar Character of the Works of Arcangelo Corelli," *Universal Magazine of Knowledge and Pleasure*, LX (April, 1777), 418.

Kruger, Walther. *Das Concerto Grosso in Deutschland*, Reinbek, 1932.

Lang, Paul Henry. *Music in Western Civilization*, New York, 1941.

Maroncelli, Pietro. "Vita di Arcangiolo Corelli," *Vite e ritratti d'illustri Italiani*, Milan, 1819.

Mishkin, Henry G. "The Solo-violin Sonata of the Bologna School," *Musical Quarterly*, January, 1943.

Monalto, Lina. "Corelli e l'Accademia dei Pamphilj," *La Scala*, No. 7, 1935.

Morini, Nestore. *Notizie di Arcangelo Corelli*, Bologna, 1913. (Extract from *L'Archiginnasio*, VIII.)

Moser, Andreas. "A. Corelli und A. Lolli," *Zeitschrift für Musikwissenschaft*, III (April, 1921).

————. "Zur Genesis der Folies d'Espagne," *Archiv für Musikwissenschaft*, 1918–19, p. 358.

————. "Zur Frage der Ornamentik in ihrer Anwendung auf Corelli's Op. V," *Zeitschrift für Musikwissenschaft*, 1918–19, p. 287.

Orsini, Luigi. *Arcangelo Corelli*, Turin, 1915.

Ortlepp, Ernst. "Corelli," *Grosses Instrumental und Vocal Concert*, XVth part, Stuttgart, 1841.

Pannain, Guido. "Arcangelo Corelli," *Rassegna Musicale*, April, 1953.

Pasini-Frassoni, F. "La Famiglia di Arcangelo Corelli," *Rivista Araldica*, V (February, 1907).

Parry, Sir Hubert H. "Corelli's Style," *Grove's Dictionary of Music*, 1928, IV, 811.

Paumgartner, B. "Corelli," *Die Musik in Geschichte und Gegenwart, fasc.* 18–19.

Persyn, Jean. "Arcangelo Corelli, l'homme et l'œuvre," *Monde musical*, August and October, 1926.

Piancastelli, Carlo. *In Onore di Arcangelo Corelli, Fusignano ad Arcangelo Corelli nel secondo centenario dalla morte, 1913,* Bologna, 1914. (A private publication by Dr. Piancastelli, who has collated in it documentation of the greatest interest concerning the biography of Corelli.)

Pincherle, Marc. "A propos de la Follia," *Revue Musicale*, April, 1923.

————. "De l'ornementation des sonates de Corelli," *Feuillets d'Histoire du violon*, Paris, 1927.

————. *Corelli*, Paris, 1933.

————. *Antonio Vivaldi et la musique instrumentale*, Paris, 1948.

———. "Comment on n'écrit pas l'histoire" (with reference to Corelli by Mario Rinaldi), *Journal Musical Français*, June 18, 1953. A review of the same work appears in the *Revue de Musicologie*, July, 1953.

Riehl, W. H. "Arcangelo Corelli im Wendepunkte zweier musikgeschichtlichen Epochen," *Sitzungsberichte der Königl. Bayer. Akad. der Wissenschaften, Philol. histor. Classe*, Munich, 1882.

Rinaldi, Mario. *Il problema degli abbellimenti nell'op. V di Corelli*, Sienna, 1947.

———. *Arcangelo Corelli*, Milan, 1953.

Sartori, Claudio. "Le quarantaquattro edizioni italiane delle sei opere di Corelli," *Rivista Musicale Italiana*, January, 1953.

Schering, Arnold. *Geschichte des Instrumentalkonzerts*, 2nd ed., Leipzig, 1927.

Smith, William C. *A Bibliography of the Musical Works Published by J. Walsh During the Years 1695–1720*, London, 1948.

Toni, Alceo. "Arcangelo Corelli," *Bollettino bibliografico musicale*, August–September, 1927.

Vaccolini, D. "Corelli," in Emilio de Tipaldo's, *Biografia degli Italiani illustri*, II, Venice, 1835.

Vatielli, Francesco. "Il Corelli e i maestri bolognesi del suo tempo," *Arte e Vita Musicale in Bologna*, I, Bologna, 1927.

———. "Le Quinte del Corelli," *Nuova Musica*, April, 1913.

ANONYMOUS SOURCES

"Arcangelo Corelli," *The Illustrated Sporting and Dramatic News*, London, March 22, 1779.

"Vita di Arcangelo Corelli Fusignano," in *Vite e ritratti di uomini celebri di tutti i tempi*, Milan, 1821.

"Memoir of A. Corelli," *The Harmonicon*, London, II (1824).

"Sketches of the Lives of Celebrated Composers: III, Arcangelo Corelli," *The Musical Magazine*, London, I (1835).

"A. Corelli und seine Sonaten," *Neue Zeitschrift für Musik*, 1873 (11 articles).

Il Liceo musicale di Santa Cecilia nel II Centenario dalla morte di Arcangelo Corelli, Rome, 1913.

Catalogo della mostra Corelliana . . . per la Celebrazione della nascita di Arcangelo Corelli Roma, Palazzo Braschi, Dicembre 1953—Gennaio 1954.

Index

231